PRAISE FOR
LEAVING THE OCD CIRCUS

Ms. Pagacz, over a period of years, has poured heart, soul, and sinew, into this book, and the result is remarkable. She describes the torment of OCD from the inside. Fellow sufferers will feel understood; families and friends will gain unique insight into what their loved one is experiencing.

Her compelling narrative abounds with powerful metaphors. Employing a creative scrapbook format, and using photos, Illustrations, and original poems, Ms. Pagacz enhances the text with a power only art can convey.

Beyond the descriptive narrative, however, is a compendium of useful information about the disorder and how to best manage it. Drawing on what worked for her, and based on researching expert advice, chapters contains a summary of useful tips and key points to remember. The result is educational and inspirational.

This memoir of her recovery is a highly valuable, unique gift to the OCD community.

DAN KALB, PHD
Psychologist, OCD specialist

LEAVING THE OCD CIRCUS

LEAVING THE OCD CIRCUS

Your Big Ticket Out of Having to Control Every Little Thing

KIRSTEN PAGACZ

Conari Press

This edition first published in 2016 by Conari Press, an imprint of
Red Wheel/Weiser, LLC
With offices at:
65 Parker Street, Suite 7
Newburyport, MA 01950
www.redwheelweiser.com

ISBN: 978-1-57324-681-1
Library of Congress Cataloging-in-Publication Data

Names: Pagacz, Kirsten, author.
Title: Leaving the OCD circus : your big ticket out of having to control
  every little thing / Kirsten Pagacz.
Other titles: Leaving the obsessive-compulsive disorder circus
Description: Newburyport, MA : Conari Press, 2016. | Includes bibliographical
  references.
Identifiers: LCCN 2016017700 | ISBN 9781573246811 (paperback)
Subjects: LCSH: Obsessive-compulsive disorder. | Obsessive-compulsive
  disorder--Treatment. | BISAC: SELF-HELP / Mood Disorders. |
PSYCHOLOGY /
  Psychopathology / Compulsive Behavior.
Classification: LCC RC533 .P25 2016 | DDC 616.85/227--dc23
LC record available at https://lccn.loc.gov/2016017700

Cover art and design by Doug Pagacz
Interior images © Kirsten Pagacz unless otherwise noted
Interior by Joseph Allen Black
josephallenblack.com
Typeset in Bell MT

Printed in the United States of America
M&G

10 9 8 7 6 5 4 3 2 1

I dedicate this book to individuals who suffer with OCD and their friends and family. I wrote this book for you. Your freedom is important to me.

To my best friend, Doug, and my loving mother, Sandra. We've shared decades together, filled with ups and downs. Thank you for your never-ending supply of love and believing in me when I struggled to believe in myself. You are forever in the biggest part of my heart.

CONTENTS

FOREWORD

When I first met Kirsten Pagacz, we were both attending the International OCD Foundation's annual conference. She had just purchased a copy of my memoir and asked me to sign it. While I can't honestly say I remember our conversation that day, I do know what I wrote just above my signature: "All things are possible when we dare to believe."

It dawns on me today, so many years later, that Kirsten's story and the very book you're now holding are powerful proof of that scribbled declaration.

There's a reason obsessive-compulsive disorder (OCD) is known as the Doubting Disease. At its core are intrusive what-if questions that can become so overwhelming sufferers will do almost anything—including performing all kinds of nonsensical rituals—in desperate attempts to relieve their anxiety. Consumed by these relentless obsessions and the compulsions they spawn, individuals with OCD find themselves doubting virtually everything, including their own abilities and judgment.

I know this from experience, having nearly lost everything to OCD many years ago, but I also know that recovery is possible—if, and only if, one dares to believe. *Belief,* after all, is the true antidote to doubt, and those with the courage to cultivate it can, in fact, do anything, including take back their lives from the grips of this debilitating disorder. Kirsten gets this, and by sharing her inspiring story in these pages she offers us not only great hope but also a reminder of the mechanics of believing—in ourselves, in others, and in life itself.

It's often said that good writing shows rather than tells, and Kirsten has done a masterful job demonstrating through her stories just what it's like to live with OCD. When she describes the agony she's in while battling an especially horrific obsession and notes that she "could no longer tell the difference between an actual situation and a thought," we are right there inside her head; and when she recounts an exposure challenge she undertakes in a grocery store, we can feel the pain and exhaustion she's fighting. Especially for those who have not experienced OCD, this kind of peek behind the curtains is truly invaluable.

As someone who stumbled through the mental health treatment world for far too long before getting into proper therapy, I find myself ever vigilant for well-intentioned but misguided information about OCD and its treatment. I can assure you that there's none of that in this book. From Kirsten's intimate depictions of obsessions and compulsions and their dysfunctional interplay (which she creatively calls "OCD math") to her detailed descriptions of exposure and response prevention treatment, the information is spot-on. That Kirsten adds to all this her insightful Key Points to Remember sections is a big bonus for readers looking for practical tools they can apply in following her path to recovery.

While there are many wonderful accounts of what it's like to live with OCD, there is something especially powerful about the message Kirsten aims to leave her readers with—a message very near and dear to me. For years I have been writing and speaking about the value of what I call Greater Good motivation. Through my own journey, and those of so many other OCD survivors I've met, I've become convinced that *purpose* and *service* are the most powerful motivators available to us when battling fear and doubt. Time and again in these pages, Kirsten makes clear that she too has discovered this, explaining, for example, why she decided to tell her story: "Helping OCD sufferers and those loved ones who are trying to understand them was my burning motivation."

When I wrote my inscription for Kirsten all those years ago, I never could have known that I'd be privileged to write those same words again at the beginning of her wonderful book. I think we can now both say with great certainty that truly *all things are possible when we dare to believe.*

JEFF BELL
Author of *Rewind, Replay, Repeat* and *When in Doubt, Make Belief*

INTRODUCTION

When I was nine, I started developing obsessive-compulsive disorder (OCD). And I lived in its grip for over twenty years. People without OCD often ask me what it feels like. Imagine you have to build a house of cards. Your OCD is the blowing fan right next to it. You can't stop yourself from building the house of cards because your brain has a hiccup, and the fan will never shut off. And, oh yeah, there is someone holding a gun to your head demanding that you perform perfectly.

Frustrating doesn't come close to describing it, but complete madness does.

I have learned how to stop building the house of cards, doing what my OCD tells me to do, and, most importantly, I have shut off the fan.

In this book I tell the story of how I learned to take down my obsessive-compulsive disorder. I will show you how to do the same thing. Yes, you heard that right. YOU are BIGGER than YOUR OCD, and of this I am sure. What's different about this book than others you may have read is that it's written not by a doctor or therapist or expert, but from the perspective of someone who has lived through the disorder—from "the street level." I've read a lot of books, met with a lot of doctors, and fought a lot of OCD battles, and this book gives me the opportunity to share with you what I've learned about what OCD is and how to work with it until you are back in charge of your life. I know it might sound cliché, but if I can do it, so can you.

OCD comes in many different forms; it all depends on the person. Some people are afraid and crippled by the thought of contaminants and are *cleaners*; others are driven to madness with the overwhelming need to be *perfect*; there are *compulsive checkers, hoarders*, and *repeaters*, also *orderers*, those who require that the things around them be arranged in a particular and rigid way; there are *thinking ritualizers*; and the list goes on from there. However, we are all human, and we are all so much more than these labels! Maybe we don't fear the same things, maybe the form of your OCD is different from mine (I experienced most of the things on that list), but we all want the same peace, don't we? That's why we do such crazy things! We're chasing that elusive mental stillness. My intention is to give you a book that is protein packed for the mind and the soul.

I constructed this book—text and pictures—to help you out of your own constriction.

I have been collecting imagery, especially vintage art and ephemera, nearly all my life. Pictures and words that really spoke to me at a core level. Some seemed to capture exactly what I was feeling. Some reminded me of pain, some of hope or freedom. I have a feeling these images and words will hit you like that, too, and I've sprinkled them like bread crumbs throughout the book to help guide you out of your dark forest or show you a different path. I want you to feel seen and heard. I hope these pictures help you feel my presence in your life. I hear you. I get you.

Sufferers will relate; the people who love us will learn. If you are an OCD hostage like I once was, or if you wish to understand and help someone who suffers from OCD, this book is for you. It's about claiming your freedom and getting your life back. If you feel alone and isolated, or know and love someone who does, this book will become a good friend and a valuable resource. We are *all* at different places on the OCD and wellness spectrum, and I wrote this book with the intention to meet you right where you are, wherever you are.

Great things are done by a series of small things brought together.

—VINCENT VAN GOGH

· 1 ·

A BUDDING RELATIONSHIP

The New Stranger and the Invitation

1975: Nine Years Old (OCD Arrives)

It was a Sunday night. I had just spent another weekend at my dad's, and he was dropping me off at my mom's red brick townhouse in Oak Park, Illinois, like he did on every other Sunday night. He had partial custody of me, so I stayed with him every other weekend, and he would come visit me once a week. Usually, we'd go to a movie or to the park to play Frisbee or something, and then we'd grab a bite to eat somewhere in Oak Park. My mom's philosophy had always been that it was better to have a father than not to have a father at all.

This townhouse was where I lived with my mom and two older brothers, Kent and Brian, from a different dad. Dad got my suitcase out of the trunk, and Mom came out to greet us. We were standing beside my dad's blue Chevy Nova. I was tired from a long weekend at his place. I was eager for them to finish talking so I could go inside.

Then I heard something like this. It came in a voice that I had never heard before. "Want to play a fun game?" this Stranger said softly, sort of in my head but kind of from above looking down at me at the same time.

I didn't answer him out loud, knowing instinctively that our communication was not for anyone else to hear. I answered him back silently: "What's the game?"

"The game is Tapping, and if you play it perfectly, you get the prize. It's simple, but it takes a lot of skill."

This piqued my interest, of course. I liked prizes. What nine-year-old doesn't?

"How do I play?"

"You tap your index finger precisely on the very same spot of the car hood with the same amount of pressure, over and over, exactly twenty-seven times with absolutely no error in your action."

Hmm, I thought, *I can do this. I'm certain of it.* I knew the prize would be mighty. I just knew it. I believed that my reward would be feeling good inside, that I would feel calm and secure, and everything would be right again. That's what I wanted more than anything, especially after a long weekend at my dad's house. "Okay," I said to the clever Stranger.

I felt so special. He'd designed this private game just for me and for no one else to see. So, as my parents continued to talk, I started my first Tapping game, the first instance of OCD behavior I remember.

I thought over the challenge one more time before I began. I would have to use the very tip of my right index finger and tap out to this certain designated number. Twenty-seven taps on the trunk of the car. My reward would come after I had done it perfectly, after I had dedicated myself to the game.

I found it exciting that the Tapping rules were so exacting, and I did not want to fail. I stared down at my index finger and started tapping. I got to nine perfectly, but on ten too much of the fatty tip of my index finger touched the car and with a bit too much pressure. Immediately the Stranger spoke. I would have to start over.

I looked over at my mom and dad to see if they were watching. They were not. I knew that if I really concentrated, without any distractions or interruptions, I could do it; I just had to apply myself better.

The Stranger watched over my shoulder to make sure I was doing it right. This game was harder than I thought. I had to start and stop at least a dozen times. I craved the moment when the Stranger would say, "At ease, soldier."

Turns out my timing wasn't too bad. Just as I successfully finished the game, my parents were wrapping up their talk. I'd won. It felt so good. I felt some sort of rewarding self-satisfaction.

Of course, I didn't know I'd be playing the Tapping game with the Stranger again.

"Bye, Dad. Love you." I grabbed my suitcase and ran to the front door of our house. Just like a normal nine-year-old. I held the screen door open for my mom.

Of course, this wasn't the only time I would hear from this Stranger. He magically seemed to know that I often felt uncomfortable and unsettled, and he knew just how to fix it: more games.

Longfellow Park 1974: Eight Years Old (Pre-OCD)

One summer day before I met OCD (which I would not know by name for another twenty years), I was at the playground by myself. I now think of that day as a kind of soul fossil. I can practically still smell and taste it. I remember how I smelled like a mixture of fresh green grass, dirt, and metal chain from the swings at the park, the top of my head baked by the sun and my hair hot and shiny. I remember the feeling of an untucked shirt, my belly round, and my knees dirty.

As a little girl I had a thirst for life you wouldn't believe. I loved how the bees would buzz around in their yellow-and-black-striped fuzzy outfits, as if they were enjoying a celebration together. I even found the flies magnificent. Their backs were colored with flowing metallic violets, blues, and greens. The colors would catch the sunlight, and I would stare at them and wonder how God made such color and put it onto their backs.

I remember hanging on to the jungle gym, which was in the shape of a submarine. I would hang and hang and hang, like a smiling monkey hanging from the limb of a tree. I hung until I felt my arms might stretch out of their sockets, but even this burning sensation felt good. My tennis shoes would create little dust clouds as my feet dangled and brushed across the gray rocks and tan pebbles.

I remember the swings. They were another land. I would sail through the air. The rushing breeze would cool my flushed face. My hands would sweat as I held on to the chains tighter and went higher. My heart would pump with excitement in my chest. I could hear it; I was alive. This was living. This was life, my life.

I could not have known that this was the best life would get. At least for a long, long time. I was calm, happy, filled with joy. I didn't need for anything.

Orange Tiger Lilies

My mom was incredibly vulnerable when she met my dad. Just before he came into the picture, she had lost a one-year-old daughter to spinal meningitis and a husband to suicide. She was raising two boys on her own and bringing in a small income, just barely making ends meet. Times were not easy. I think my dad brought in that fresh air she was looking for.

Things were not what they seemed, though. My dad cheated on her, was mentally abusive to her and my brothers, and had begun doing drugs like acid, mescaline, and pot. My mom and dad divorced when I was about two and a half.

After the divorce, my dad lived in a one-bedroom cottage near the Fox River in Illinois. It was not built for year-round living. It was a small summer house that was painted dirty white and had black-framed windows.

This was the 1970s, and my dad's horn-rimmed glasses and plaid shorts had given way to hippie beads and Nehru shirts. My mom has since said that she thought he looked a lot like Michael Douglas.

At the time of my parents' divorce, the court ordered that my dad could come for visits every Thursday. Usually, we would go to the park or a movie, or get something to eat. I also had to stay with my dad every other weekend and for three consecutive weeks during the dead August heat of a Chicago summer. This was my dad's time off from teaching sociology at the local community college.

Due to the constant moisture in the air because the house was near the river, the wooden doors were warped and never closed just right between rooms. The front porch always smelled like mildew and mold from the hundreds of stacked books that were trapped with moisture. Out front to the right and left of the steps, orange tiger lilies would bloom in late spring. They were wild looking and came up with the weeds. I have never grown an affinity for orange tiger lilies.

There was no air-conditioning in the house, just one large beige-and-white box fan that didn't do a good job of cooling the place. It just pushed the warm air around, and I spent a lot of my time sitting in front of it trying to cool myself off. This is when I happily discovered, like many kids do, that if I talked directly into the fan, my voice would sound really funny. Fortunately, this activity created some entertainment and helped me pass the time. I spent a lot of the mornings and early after-noons trying to entertain myself while waiting for my dad to get up after another late night of his doing drugs and more than likely visiting random friends.

For years I stayed hopeful that one of these mornings he would wake up and want to play a game with me. I remember whispering in my dad's ear, "Daddy, Daddy. When are you going to get up?" And he would say, in a quiet mumble with his face in the pillow, "Oh honey, just give me a little longer." His little longer was always a big longer. It was clear that he just wasn't available. I could feel sadness filling me up like smoke fills a room.

Most people would say that my dad's bedroom was really in his living room, the main space in the center of his house. There were a couple of maroon-colored Chianti bottles on the floor that he used as candleholders. A rainbow of colorful drips of melted wax stuck to the bottles. When I was bored, sometimes I would pick them off.

This was where my dad and his girlfriend, who was once one of his students, slept on the mattress in the middle of the floor. Her skin was clean and fresh looking, and I thought she was very natural looking and very pretty. Her wavy dark brown hair was long, more than halfway down her back and parted straight down the middle. She was eighteen and looked to me like a high schooler; he was well into his thirties.

After he brought her into our picture, I had to ride in the backseat of his car every time we all went somewhere. At that time, I believed I was his number three. First came his drugs, parties, and music; second was the girlfriend; and then third, me.

On the back of the living room/bedroom wall was a huge photographic mural of an autumn scene filled with brown-, gold-, and orange-leaved trees and a dusty, winding road in the middle. Sometimes I would stare at it and imagine walking right into the wall and down that road. How I wish I could have done exactly that!

My dad frequently walked around his house naked. I think my mom asked him once not to do it with me there, and he said something like, "It's my house, and if I want to walk around naked, that's what I'm going to do. There's nothing about the human body to be ashamed of." His girlfriend, at least, was modest enough to cover herself with a thin T-shirt that reached her upper thighs. But every time she bent over to get into a cabinet or pick up something, there to greet me was this horrible-looking thing. It looked like a loose pile of rare roast beef and scared the hell out of me. It was her droopy vagina! In my young mind I was afraid I was going to fall into it if I looked at it for more than a split second. When I grew up, would I have one of those, too? The thought petrified me.

Because he was a professor at a community college, my dad had access to the best audio-visual equipment the '70s had to offer, so in his living room he would put on quite a show for what seemed like an endless and steady stream of his drugged-up friends. Some became familiar around the house, but there were always some new faces. A constant stream of drugs and young people mostly with long hair.

My dad used to say he wanted to "lose his mind" on psychedelics.

I would watch as he and everyone else got high. I remember learning how to pass a joint from one person to another while sitting in a communal circle in the living room. I wasn't in it, exactly, but I was a part of it. A silent witness.

I clearly remember hearing the loud screams of the lady on Pink Floyd's *Dark Side of the Moon* and being scared half to death. My dad, his girlfriend, and their friends lay on the floor watching a 16 mm film of pulsating geometric shapes projected on the white sheet my dad put up in front of the mural. I guess they were trying to lose their minds. The music was turned up so loud that my ears stung in pain and my head pounded.

Exhausted, I would go into my tiny bedroom and try to fall asleep.

This kind of scene was repeated every weekend.

I would pull the thin, musky sheet over my head and cry myself to sleep. Sometimes when I couldn't take it anymore, I would find him in the carnage and beg him to turn down the music.

He never did. Not once.

Our Secret Friendship Grows (The Games) — 1975: Nine Years Old

There was nothing I could do about my dad's crazy, drug-fueled life or my mom's busy work schedule and the late hours her demanding job required, but I could tap. I could tap, and the chaos inside me would stop—at least for a little while.

I started playing the Tapping game more and more. I tapped in school, at home, anywhere. I tapped on my favorite green corduroy pants, the kitchen countertop, a stranger's parked car, my school folder—no place was off-limits for the game. I even tapped on Angela, my Siamese cat, which was especially hard because she was a living target and rarely stayed perfectly still. It would take me a long time to tap correctly on her soft and smooth fur.

Of course, the Stranger was always there, always judging.

The Tapping game was especially hard if it was at a higher number, like thirty-two or forty-five. Sometimes I would have to chase Angela around the house or pull her out from under a chair or the couch so that I could finish tapping on her back. Sometimes, if she was particularly unhappy with me, she would puncture me with her pointy fangs, but I would work through it. I had to.

A substantial portion of people do what they are told to do, irrespective of the content of the act and without limitations of conscience, so long as they perceive that the command comes from a legitimate authority.

**DR. STANLEY MILGRAM,
IN *THE SOCIOPATH NEXT DOOR*
BY MARTHA STOUT**

Eventually, once the Stranger thought I'd gotten good enough at Tapping, he graduated me to some new challenges. By this time, however, he was sounding more like a military sergeant. He spoke with a soft voice, but he was very, very insistent and there was an omnipotent quality about him, too—there to make sure I did everything correctly and to code—and to keep me company like a friend.

Cleaner Is Better for Sergeant and Me (OCD Is Morphing)

As a child, I believed that a pure, good, and perfect life looked something like the household cleaning commercials that I saw on TV. Some lucky kid's mom is so happy and looks so nice. She steps into her sunny kitchen after using Mr. Clean on her floors and counters. She's smiling and relieved. Her kitchen is spotless, bright, and clean. All I could think was that she was so lucky to have met her goal and her kids were equally fortunate. That TV world looked so ideal; it appealed to me on a deep level.

My bedroom was my world, and I had goals, too. I kept it to the maximum clean, just like in a TV commercial: tidy, straightened, dusted, and polished. I controlled this environment. Anything less was just not right. I no longer accepted uncleanliness and disorganization, and, more importantly, neither did the Sergeant, who was no longer soft-spoken at all.

I had a "socks-only" drawer. All of my socks had to be folded exactly the same way, into tight little perfectly round balls. They had to face the same way and line up perfectly, side by side, in color-specific rows. If a sock was not rolled right, I would unroll it and roll it back up again until it was. This felt critical to my well-being.

Under Sergeant's command, I controlled a sterile and perfect environment. I controlled all the objects and all the space between the objects. The lamp had its perfect position on the table. I made the bed the exact same way every day. The sheets were tucked in tight, and the top sheet was folded and creased perfectly to a straight edge. Nothing out of place, ever! Nothing dusty, ever! I lived by a doctrine of complete and utter order, Sergeant Style. Commanding the order of things on the outside made me feel better on the inside. The reward was intrinsic.

My mother didn't seem to notice that anything was wrong. She was thrilled that I was so neat. I was like a waitress in a diner, constantly taking care of her station. Wiping down tables and straightening the salt, pepper, sugar, and creamer; I had to control all the elements. Things started to *have to* be a certain way or I would feel off inside and uncomfortable.

Keeping up was exhausting, but the rewards made it all worthwhile.

One day, while recleaning my room, it suddenly occurred to me that inside and at the top of my bedroom closet there was a bright and bare lightbulb that I'd never dusted. Sergeant was right there to show me who was boss: "Because that bulb has never been dusted, your room has never been absolutely perfect and clean," he said as if through clenched teeth.

I sank into disappointment. That was all I needed to hear. My room was no longer perfect. It was tainted, contaminated. Clearly, this disturbing situation would have to be rectified immediately. Thoughts of this impure, dusty bulb way up high in my closet filled my mind. I was edgy and distraught. Nothing was going to stand between me and that dusty lightbulb. Nothing!

This was the '70s and pretend kitchen sets were the rave for little girls. I was lucky to have one. My mini kitchen table set was badass; it had four little chairs with shiny vinyl leopard-print seats—the coolest. When I was in the mood for entertaining, I would often set one of my Siamese cats on one of the chairs and turn on my 45 rpm record player. My cats never stayed too long; they never made it through a whole song. But I was glad, if only for a little bit.

Back to the scene of the crime, I dragged one of the leopard-print chairs over to my closet. My plan was to stand up tall on the chair and dust the bulb and its white metal base. With Windex in one hand and a clean, soft cloth in the other, I ventured upward toward the unclean bulb, but no matter how much I stretched, I could not reach it.

Next, I gathered some large books from my bookshelf. Of course, all the books were lined up in order from smallest on the left to largest on the right. I stacked some of the books on my chair and climbed up. But even after standing on the books, I was still not tall enough to reach the impure bulb.

I could not disappoint Sergeant. It was important that I was obedient. He did not like to be kept waiting.

That's when I spied my gerbil tank. It looked to be just about the extra height I needed to reach the bulb.

I loved my two little gerbils. They were my cute little friends, and I loved to watch them play in the wood shreds and curls. To shield them from my cats and thus a potentially terrible fate, I'd always kept a piece of heavy glass on top of their tank, leaving a small opening so fresh air could get in but our three Siamese cats could not.

With all my strength, I got my arms around the tank and carried it over to the chair. All right, everything was coming together now. I had the chair, the books, and the glass container. Really, this plan seemed like a stroke of brilliance.

I took the stack of books off the chair and put the gerbil aquarium on it. I then slid the heavy piece of glass over to completely cover the top. I knew I'd be quick and efficient and my little guys would have more air soon. Then came the books in their perfect stack.

I had no trouble climbing up my well-thought-out stack of items. Windex and a soft cotton cloth in hand, I made it to the top, standing with my feet aquarium-width apart so as not to break the glass.

My Windex was opened, and I had it on spray. As soon as I aimed at the bulb and sent out the first squirt, I started to feel relief. Wipe, wipe, wipe the dusty bulb with the cloth. The situation was looking promising.

But Sergeant wasn't satisfied. He barked, "This job is not good enough. You need to take the bulb out of its metal base and spray into the hole where the bulb goes in. The whole area needs to be clean, not just the meager little bulb!" Craving some peace of mind, I knew I'd have to do as he said; there was no other choice. This time Sergeant really went for it. "If you ever wish to be loved again by your family, you have to complete this task."

So, with the cloth covering my hand, I unscrewed the hot bulb and took it out of the hole. I could feel its heat through the cloth. I aimed the Windex directly into the hole and squirt, squirt, squirted the spray right in. Then, with cloth-wrapped fingers, I reached into the hole and began to wipe.

The electrical charge hurled me to the floor. From the tips of my fingers, the electricity surged through my body and straight into my toes. I landed on my back—the books, aquarium, and chair thrown in all directions.

Lying there on the floor, unable to move, I was certain that I had been electrocuted and died, like the boy I'd heard about who lost his life on the train tracks. So I kept my eyes closed for a little while. I thought that I should wait for my angels to come get me and take me to heaven.

When the angels hadn't come after a few minutes, I thought that maybe I'd gone straight to heaven. I cautiously opened my eyes. *Wow,* I thought, *How funny! Heaven looks just like my bedroom; maybe they are welcoming me with something familiar.* The dizzying effects from the fall started to wear off, and eventually I sat up and looked straight ahead into my closet. One end of the glass top had come down hard during the fall and was now inside the tank.

I got up and slowly walked over to take a closer look. The situation was awful: the glass, like a guillotine, had chopped into the exact same spot on the back of the gerbils' necks, and their eyes had popped out and were still attached to purple tendons. It looked like a scene from a horror movie. I couldn't believe what I saw, and I felt so guilty.

I could feel the complete silence of my bedroom, and a deep, over-whelming grief—not only because this had happened but because I had done it. I had killed my little friends.

Oddly enough, Sergeant wasn't angry. In fact, he was reassuring. "Don't worry too much; you did the right thing. After all, the bulb had to be cleaned." Sergeant spoke with an incredible confidence, and I believed him.

As awful as I felt about my little guys meeting a terrible death at my hands, I also felt so good that the hole under the lightbulb was now clean and dust-free, that the lightbulb was spotless, and that the Sergeant was pleased with me. The reward of pleasing Sergeant was just about the best thing ever. And for the next twenty-three years, I did whatever he asked, no matter how strange it got.

Although I don't remember exactly, after my electrocution, I most likely headed outside to look for someone to play with in the neighborhood.

I was lucky; my neighborhood was loaded with kids, and a lot of them were close in age. If I was particularly lucky that day, my best friend Victoria, who lived a few doors down in the same townhouse, could come out and play. Maybe we would have cartwheel competitions on our neighbor's front lawn, or we'd get Oana, a girl whose family came from Romania, to come out and play, too; this way, we'd have more judges and contestants for our cartwheel competitions. Or to scrounge together some change, we could return my mom's Tab soda bottles at the neighborhood grocery store that was a couple of blocks away. Then we'd buy red licorice for ourselves and start eating it in the alley on the walk back home.

Usually, there was a game of Kick the Can starting up somewhere, or we'd jump on our bikes and go exploring. We were really living all right, and we came home with dirty, grass-stained pants and sometimes a hole in the knee from a rough landing while doing bicycle ballet.

Today I am grateful for growing up in this neighborhood and all my memories of the great adventures that took place between the mulberry trees and the old oaks. Growing up there, on the south side of Oak Park, gave me a really solid base, a core of joy.

Even though Sergeant was bobbing in and out—that was how my OCD worked at this time—there were even stretches when Sergeant seemed to take most of the day off.

Photo: Victoria Moran/Illustration by the author

I need a "pure experience", nothing less.

Schlage Opens the Way—
1977: Eleven Years Old

Like an exploding firecracker, and just as exciting, the clock did its final yell for the day. School was out. Many kids went home to their mom or somebody waiting for them at their front door. When I got home, I was alone for a while. Sometimes our front door was wide open when I arrived home, which scared me. Other times, the door was locked, and I had to use the Schlage key that hung on the thick red yarn around my neck. The reason I knew Schlage was written on the key was that every day I held the key very close in front of my eyes and stared at that one mysterious word, *Schlage*, engraved into the golden metal.

"Stare at that word and not at the edges of the key. If you do see the edges, start over!" the Sergeant yelled at me.

Of course, I had to do what he said. Sergeant commanded me to stop completely, even stop breathing when I stared at his chosen word. I fell into a trance, like I'd been hypnotized. I had to dissolve myself and fall into the word, so I was the word and nothing else existed. I had to do this so that Sergeant would clear me to pass into the next second of my life. He decided when I got to go forward.

I also knew the words on the toilet and bathtub because I stared at them a lot: *Foster*. Only when I had a Pure Experience would Sergeant let up on me a bit. My body would get to feel right, all parts, but only briefly until the next task.

If the neighborhood kids weren't home from their school yet, I would probably spend some time indoors with my three Siamese cats. Sometimes my brother Brian, who's four years older than me, would be in the neighborhood somewhere goofing around with his friends. Sometimes I was included, but some days I was not. My other brother, Kent, who's ten years older than me, was probably at that electronics shop, fixing broken TVs. I'd seen this place that he went to, and I was particularly fond of the flickering red neon sign out front that created a moodiness, especially on a dark rainy night.

Sixth Grade Summer

By the summer after sixth grade, I had been obeying Sergeant for a few years. He did help me in many ways. When I was feeling lonely, he was there for me. He helped me do things the right way, and not the wrong way, which was very important. Mostly, I think, he was a good friend. He kept me occupied and away from boredom. He was my only ticket to calm. When I began to feel uncomfortable with people, myself, and my surroundings, he always showed up and was always on time with something for me to do.

I started "reporting" to the Sergeant on a regular basis. The more I performed for him, the more powerful he became.

On those rare times that I tried to defy him or, worse yet, disobey him and not do as he demanded, this resulted in my immediate punishment. I was instantly overcome with unbridled anxiety, nausea, and panic, my face flushed with rashes; my head pounded; and my heart raced. I learned early on that it was just easier to do all the tasks and achieve his approval and not have to deal with the alternative—those unbearable and overwhelming feelings of pure discomfort. The tasks just became a part of the mix of my daily life, what I had to do in an effort to maintain some kind of stability and—even bigger than that— my important contribution to universal order; there was almost a magical and transcendent quality about me doing things right.

Sergeant frequently gave me mandatory sporadic drills that involved repetition like tapping, staring, cleaning, swallowing, blinking, and now checking. In a weird way, these drills were almost soothing, like rocking in a chair. But now, there was more at stake and tied to the tasks than my overall comfort. He warned me about all the bad things that would happen and pointed out all the potential threats and doom that would come if I did not do what I was told to do! Sergeant had a direct route into my mind and would fill it with terrifying thoughts and images. It was as though he could project a stream of horrific movies in my head and use my creativity against me.

If I didn't perform and complete a task, he told me that I would be responsible for fires, deaths, and that was just the beginning. It's like we had an agreement: If I did everything right, the way he instructed, no matter how seemingly odd, then everything would be okay. I would temporarily feel right in myself, and this is what I intrinsically craved. Just to feel okay was a rare luxury, and Sergeant knew this.

On this day we were in the kitchen. "If you don't check the dials on the stove again, your cats will die!" My brain filled with lightning. I didn't want my cats to die! Sergeant had both my full attention and emotional buy-in. Of course, I would do anything to save my cats, my loving and furry friends, from death. I did what Sergeant told me to do in a brave attempt to stop the inevitable future suffering of those I loved.

I quickly learned that Sergeant was an authority figure and the epicenter for dishing out punishment and doling out rewards. He had a certain sort of power because he was coming from inside my own head sort of, which made him seem much more convincing.

It's clear that we pay attention to authority figures and direct our attention toward what they deem important out of either fear or respect, depending on the type of authority they wield.

—BEN PARR, *CAPTIVOLOGY*

"No, no, I checked the stove," I tried to reassure Sergeant.

"How do you know that you really checked it? You might just think that you did, and you know your track record. You've done stupid things before. You make stupid mistakes all the time!"

"Okay, I'll check it again."

"Your cats are going to die if you don't!"

After a perfect performance, I felt so good, sort of like a superhero. I saved my cats from impending doom, and momentarily I felt that I had a little power myself, saving them and all.

Pretty soon, checking the burners on the stove, in a perfect and precise way, was just one of those things I had to do every night before going to bed and every time I left the house. It was just the way it was and just way too weird to tell anyone. It never once dawned on me that I had an illness with a name. I chalked it all up to being a weird kid: me, Sergeant, my games, my drills, my tasks, my performances. It's just the way we were, and I accepted it. Okay, maybe I knew I was a little broken way deep down inside, but what could I do?

My brother Brian called me Kirsten Weirdsten, sometimes with a teasing tone. He found my creativity an undesirable character flaw. That was the Weirdsten part. We had different dads and our minds worked differently. He, like my oldest brother, has the mind of an engineer, and I have the mind of a sensitive poet; we just come at things differently. I also felt like he was always trying to control me, and I wanted none of it. I already had one Sergeant to report to, thank you. I knew that letting anyone know about Sergeant would make me even more Kirsten Weirdsten. I knew that if I told anyone about Sergeant, he would yell in my face until the end of time and I'd be forced into a straitjacket and taken to a mental hospital where people get locked up for life.

Sergeant Style

Perfecting, tapping, staring, checking, cleaning, transferring, dieting, blinking, swallowing—the challenge was to do all of these things with no one noticing. Sergeant and I had numerous covert operations.

It was a new school year: 1978. Feathered hair was still a big trend. My brown hair was short, feathered in layers, and swooshed back. I had the Kristy McNichol cut, and I loved it. (She played the youngest daughter on a hit TV show called *Family*.)

By now, Sergeant and I were a highly functional and exacting team; after all, he demanded perfection. I was an A student and was ready for any challenge. In my back pocket, resting on my rear and sometimes poking me in the butt, were my perfectly sharpened—like surgical tools—number-two pencils. I was ready for any test by any teacher at any given time. I was focused on doing well.

I didn't like the lead residue left on my hands after sharpening my pencils; but I couldn't always go wash my hands immediately after. By not washing, I felt as though I was not finishing my task to full completion, and this bothered me. I would think about the "transfer of residue" to other things that I touched. This could lead to an infinite amount of "transfer." I would be responsible for adding invisible grime to the universe. This made me feel guilty that I wasn't cleaner—not to mention the terrible stink of a sawmill that I had with me. In class I would think about my stinky hands over and over again, and I couldn't seem to get them out of my mind and stop worrying about them. If I only could have washed my hands!

This inability to forget unfinished tasks is known as the Zeigarnik effect [who knew!].

—BEN PARR, *CAPTIVOLOGY*

Boobs

My boobs looked different in the bathtub and when I was changing my top. I looked down. "Yikes! These are weird." I poked at one of them to see what it would do. My boobs didn't really look very booby-ish; they looked like tiny, pointy, stretched-out white balloons with light pink-colored tips. Yuck! They looked like they had started growing and abruptly stopped. I could really see why my mom thought I should cover mine up with a training bra at first. I was on board with this idea; the faster I could cover them, the better.

I didn't like the dark brown hairs showing up on my lady area either; they made me feel more wrong. My dad liked to talk to me about my vagina and about me becoming a woman. He said he'd throw a party for me when I got my period; this way everyone would know I was a woman. I was very uncomfortable when he talked to me like that.

Sergeant offered me a place where my boobs didn't exist anymore; where my dad couldn't frighten me with his talks, drugs, and loud music; a place where I was not left alone in the house waiting for my mom to come home from work, where I was no longer Kirsten Weirdsten.

Temporary Euphoria

The summer I was twelve, I underwent a metamorphosis. I heard my brother and his friends talking about chicks being "foxy," and I was certain that this was my new bull's-eye. Achieving foxy would bring me the peace I had been working to achieve with Sergeant for the past several years. If I could get foxy, I would be accepted and happy and would no longer feel like a walking bruise.

I started wearing tighter, more revealing clothes, lots of makeup, and big 1980s hair. I experimented with the frosty blue Maybelline eyeliner that I saw models in the magazines wearing.

I started hanging out with the young wolves in the alley. There would often be a gang of them slouching against garbage cans, staring at their dirty gray sneakers, kicking rocks, smoking cigarettes in their army jackets, or sitting on the broken pavement in front of a garage, not necessarily their own. Let's just say none of these kids had school spirit or were particularly popular, but I thought they were cool, living on the fringe and not caring much about anything.

We wolves (because now I was one of them) would smoke bowls of pot that looked like tiny branches, golden or red hairs, clumps of dirt, and seeds that would crackle and snap when they were lit. We would smoke a few puffs, cough violently, and keep passing the joint around, our eyes glassing over and turning pink. No one seemed to give a fuck, and to me this felt pretty good. Smoking pot gave me some relief and letup from Sergeant. Plus, I loved the sensation of floating and laughing at silly things. Sergeant was barking out orders more and more these days, and I wanted to silence him. The pot delivered.

We wolves had something else in common: we all had time on our hands. We didn't have places to be, like the dinner table, and we didn't have anyone looking for us. When I was high, even though I never felt totally right, I didn't feel as wrong either.

However, one time while stoned, my braces were bothering me so much that I couldn't stand them in my mouth a second longer. The hard wires in the back were poking inside my soft, fleshy cheek. I couldn't stop thinking about them, obsessing about them and the pain they caused. Sergeant helped me to come to this conclusion and presented a winning end goal: "comfort." I decided that I had to take them off myself with a variety of tools I found at my friend's house. It's embarrassing to say this now, but one of the tools that worked especially well was a pair of toe-nail clippers. I hope I washed them before I gave myself dental surgery! I know, gross. However, they were the perfect tool for hunkering down and pulling out the wire. After I pulled out the wires the best that I could, I picked off the metal boxes glued to my teeth. My determination to get them off was greater than the pain I felt taking them off. In a driven panic, I almost got rid of every piece. The orthodontist was in shock the next time he saw me. I'm sure my mom didn't like the bill, either!

When eighth grade started, I had such a bad attitude that all seven of my teachers called a conference with my mother and said, "What happened to your daughter?!" It seemed as though nobody knew.

Not only had my personality done a 180, but we'd also moved closer to the high school I'd soon be attending because my mom had found a good deal on a condo. That well-traveled and well-known land of my old neighborhood had now evaporated into the distant past "when I was a kid." I was becoming a teenager, and that meant no more kid stuff. No more climbing trees with Victoria and talking to caterpillars. No more days of walking out the front door without any makeup on.

OCD LIKE A BRUSH FIRE

High School (Checker Maximus!)
OCD: 1980–1984

Then came the first day of high school. I was out the door and on my way there, to this school that was so big it looked and felt like an airport. I was about to spend the next four years of my life there. I was a bundle of nerves when I heard Sergeant say, "Are you sure you locked the door?"

"Oh my God, I didn't. What a stupid idiot I am!" I raced home.

The door was locked. I jiggled the knob again and again and said out loud, "The door is locked, the door is locked," hoping that saying it would make it stick so I didn't have to be questioned again.

But no sooner had I gotten a step away than Sergeant asked again, "Are you *sure* it's locked? How do you really know? You have made many mistakes before; you make them constantly. You should really check it one more time. The safety of your family is at stake here! [There's that emotional buy-in.] A man with a sharp knife could hide inside your condo, and the first family member to walk in . . . **SLASH!** And it would be your fault. Do you want to come home to a **BLOOD BATH and a LOVED ONE with a SLASHED THROAT?**"

I sure didn't want that; I believed every word Sergeant said to me, even though sometimes what he said went beyond my logical mind. The more I tried to resist him, the more violent his visuals became, like a slide show of blood and horror. I didn't know what else to do but comply.

I checked and relocked the door more than fifty times before I was free to go.

Finally, I was on my way to school. I was wearing my new Gloria Vanderbilt jeans that I had to zip up with a clothes hanger because they were so tight and so foxy. I remember touching my barrette several times in a certain way, making sure it was perfectly straight in my hair. Sergeant had already reminded me that if my barrette looked lopsided and sloppy, it would be a very poor reflection of me.

I needed to be sharp, with it, together, and perfect, so I straightened it again. Then I smoked several cigarettes to get some relief from the anxiety of the newness up ahead and of Sergeant breathing down my neck.

When I got to the entrance, I saw some faces I recognized from grade school. What I would've really liked to do was run up to them and yell, "Can you fuckin' believe how big this place is?" But I knew that would be childish. Excitement is for children.

I couldn't stop judging myself. If Sergeant wasn't doing it, I could fill in like a champ.

I saw a pack of perfect girls together. They apparently didn't have a bad case of "heredity" like I did, with short legs and heavy thighs. My mom always reminded me of this, and I carried it forward. One girl seemed so perfect and untouchable. She seemed to be perched like a beautiful red bird at the top of a tall pine tree, looking down, like a queen looks down at her court. Life looked so easy for her. I knew—at least right then, anyway—I wasn't worthy of her greatness. As I walked by her, pieces of me seemed to be falling off.

For me, high school was no Normal Rockwell painting. No long weekends at the football games, bake sales for special causes, or homecoming floats. I was not playing on the tennis team or working hard on the yearbook council. I spent a great deal of time in my head. What I was working hard at was trying to present a "normal front" to everybody I encountered—and keeping my relationship with Sergeant a secret.

I have heard people say that they loved high school. Clearly, they lived on a different planet than I did. For me, it went by agonizingly slow, and my list of my imperfections was endless, like a bottomless sea. Sergeant was always pointing things out and comparing me to other girls: "She's thinner than you. She's smarter than you. She fits in much better than you." I just felt wrong both inside and out and severely inadequate.

This was perfect kindling for depression. Sergeant was always in my ear, rattling off the things that made me less than acceptable, and that special place of "wonderfulness and ease" that I dreamed about was always just beyond me. I could get there if I could just be a little bit better.

> **The promise of heaven is great even if I had to go through hell to get there, it has to be worth it.**
>
> **—ROB BELL, *LOVE WINS***

One day Sergeant ordered me to look over at another girl and then said, "Oh, look, she's so tan. Too bad you're so pale white and disgusting! You need a St. Tropez tan [a popular tanning oil at the time]; you need to get some Coppertone tan lines."

After school that afternoon, I climbed up onto a friend's roof (with her approval). I lay there on a giant piece of tinfoil, dowsed in baby oil. Being fair skinned, I didn't tan. I burned to a crisp like a sizzling piece of bacon. Not quite the perfect bronze picture that I was going for.

Sergeant was quick to say, "Fail!"

Cord Check Time

Then came the cord checking. Before leaving the house, I had to do my cord checks. I would crawl around on the carpet checking the television and lamp cords. I would straighten them with my hands and lay them just the way they had to be laid, straight, from the outlet to the object. I would tug gently on them and smooth out every ripple. If every cord in the house was not lying perfectly straight, I would become unbearably agitated and couldn't leave the house.

This ritual could take me an hour, and there were many, many start-overs. In my Mental Movie, my unforgivable negligence would result in an electrical fire and the whole condo burning down and innocent people being killed. Let's just say Sergeant had my ear and undivided attention. I wanted to save people from harm.

Cord checking—and doing it right— ensured that I would avoid all potential threats. Sergeant repeated over and over to me that the cords had to be checked perfectly, and nothing else would do. His badgering was monotonous, like a metronome, and I would do just about anything to get it to stop.

Even though [repetition] had no impact on the validity, its cognitive bias is called the illusion-of-truth effect and it's a powerful effect of clever agenda setting. If something is repeated to you often enough you will start believing it's true.

—ADAPTED FROM BEN PARR'S,
CAPTIVOLOGY

If I had girlfriends over before school, I would try to do a superfast cord check, hoping they didn't notice. Of course, they'd often bust me doing this and laugh at me. They even nicknamed me "Cord Checker." They got lots of laughs out of this, and I chuckled with them trying to make light of my strange behavior. They couldn't have known that for me cord checking was a life-or-death matter.

The leaving-the-house ritual became so onerous that I was frequently late to school. The hall pass lady knew my first name and how to spell it *correctly*. For every time I was late to school, I made up a different story. The cat had gotten out. An important phone call had come just as I was leaving. My mom needed me to wait for the refrigerator repairman. Forgot my books, left my curling iron on, forgot my lunch—you get the idea. Lying to the hall pass lady was just one of the thousands of lies I told throughout my "Sergeant Cover-Up" days.

I became a crafty liar and a damn good actress. Sometimes I would cut class and go back to my house and start over with the cord checking, especially if I couldn't tolerate seeing Sergeant hold up my mom's melting face in front of me, sort of like cue cards of what would happen if

I didn't do my drills. This was incredibly motivating. While I was there with my cords, Sergeant might add something like straightening couch cushions and throw pillows.

Perfectionism is exhausting.

—MADELEINE L'ENGLE

The great painter Salvador Dali is quoted as saying, "Have no fear of perfection. You will never reach it."

Cleaning Time

Then I started forcing myself to clean. I would clean and scrub down the refrigerator and the vegetable and fruit crisper compartments over and over again. I would convince myself that tiny pieces of green lettuce were stuck in between the shelves and behind the crisper where I could not reach. All that I could think about and see were tiny and stuck pieces of lettuce, and that was making my cleaning job a failure. Sergeant would show me a visual flash card of the stuck lettuce and it said, "**FAILED!**" The lettuce would be another fine example of my deep imperfection and negligence.

My cleaning might have made the house look great, but on the inside it was hell.

Dating Time

Once a very popular guy a year older than me asked me to go to a movie with him. I don't even remember what it was. I sat frozen through the whole movie, staring straight ahead as though seeing through and beyond the screen. I was in my little trance, doing what was now a daily caloric intake drill: One strawberry Pop Tart equals 200 calories, a glass of milk is 120. I added up everything to see where I was that day. When I completed that day, I went back and did the same thing for the day before.

A couple of times during the movie, I sort of mumbled my number of calories out loud. When he said, "What?" I replied as normally as I could, "Oh nothing." We were completely not sharing the same experience.

To make matters worse, before he drove me home, he pulled the car over and parked on a street in north Oak Park that was dimly lit with lampposts. This I knew instinctively was our time to make out. I really didn't know what I was doing, but I knew that this was the time to be foxy. I had seen that when people in movies make out, sometimes the girl writhes around all seductive-like and moaning. Just like everything else, I tended to overdo it. I was like an unbridled bucking bronco kicking around in a yellow station wagon.

That boy never asked me out again, and this was just more proof of my imperfection.

Crank It Up a Notch

In the animal kingdom, especially with dogs, a fixation is an indication of an unbalanced mind and an unbalanced mind is a sign of weakness. Dogs attack weakness if they sense weakness.

—CESAR MILLAN, *THE DOG WHISPERER*

For a very brief time I went out with another popular boy in my high school. This guy, I really fell for. His aloof attitude, shiny jet-black Elvis hair and overall good looks made me feel like I needed to work even harder for his approval. Well, he lost interest in me, and I got dumped. He moved on quickly and easily. Of course, girls tend to obsess about these things more than boys do, but I absolutely could not move on. I became stuck in the thick tar of rejection. This boy not wanting me was an indisputable sign of my imperfection, right? If I didn't fix this, it would set the stage for my entire life! My world with Sergeant was black and white, no in between.

Leave it to Sergeant to swoop in with new taunts. The more I obsessed about being dropped like a sack of potatoes, the louder Sergeant got: "If you were smarter, more exotic, more interesting and beautiful, he would want you. But you are just not any of those things. I can't blame him. You have bad heredity, and that mixed with your ongoing stupidity is *so* undesirable." I didn't merely have to suffer the excruciating insecurities of being a teenaged girl; I had to endure Sergeant, too. It was all too much.

I can practically hear you saying, "Enough. I don't want to hear about Sergeant anymore." Believe me, I don't want to spend too much time on him either, best buddy. Just bear with me, though.

The plot thickens: The guy who broke up with me had a chum, and they were frequently seen together. A high school frick and frack situation.

I think the way these two boys interlocked with Sergeant is worth talking about. Precisely because I was a victim to Sergeant, first and foremost, I was that much more of an easy target to other *mental bullies*. Maybe you've been there, too.

Sergeant explained it like this: "The only way you'll know you really count in this world is if your unrequited love comes back and takes an interest in you. **That's the *only* way!**" There was no other alternative.

And I foolishly anointed these two as the authorities on my self-worth—or lack of it. They strutted around school and Oak Park as if they were in an exclusive club that only they knew about. And, of course, I saw their rejection as another **clear** reflection of my imperfection. Somehow I made getting acceptance from them everything, and they, both extremely intelligent cats, knew it.

What do young boys do when they know they have something to poke at that will react? They poke at it. Me? Unfortunately, I let them live in my head rent-free! I allowed them to avoid me, ignore me, laugh in my direction like I was a big joke, tell secrets when I was around, and openly reject me.

How I wish now that I could have said, "You two are assholes! I'm not a fucking punch line!" and called it a day. But I couldn't do that. I sucked in their collective rejection of me, and Sergeant drove it home.

It always felt that if I could just try a little harder or do things a little better, everything would be okay.

My closest girlfriend at the time knew what was going on and tried to help. With her help, she knew I could get the boy to take me back. She, I, and (secretly to me only) Sergeant were on a mission.

We would talk about improving our appearance just to "feel better." She'd say things like, "How about some blonde highlights? That'll make you feel better." Or we would focus on updating our clothes. "Let's go to Madigan's at North Riverside and get some new outfits. Don't you want to look cute tomorrow?" While we were there, "Let's get some long fake nails put on; those are sexy." In addition, we both thought losing some weight would make us look "more happening," so we went on a diet. I actually wrote a letter to myself saying that I could lose weight but not get carried away (this was an example of a good worry coming from my healthy self!). I signed it at the bottom and dated it like a contract. I don't remember if my girlfriend signed it or not, but I am fairly certain I communicated it to her.

Getting thin, now this was the target in the middle of the bull's-eye for a girl with OCD (still unbeknownst to me). I started out allowing myself a thousand calories a day and then over time got that number down very low. Scary low. Meanwhile, my girlfriend and I continued to plot new strategies for me to become more appealing to the boy who dumped me.

If she saw the two boys together, she would tell me as though she had the biggest news on the planet. Unfortunately for me, she did. I would feed on her words.

We would check our hair and makeup often, so we'd always be ready to run into them. I would curl my hair before school, and I even started bringing my curling iron to school to redo it if necessary.

The bangs were all it. If the bangs were fucked up, I knew that would make it that much more apparent how ugly my face was. I would stare at myself in the mirror and wonder why God had to make me so ugly. Now and then, when I was feeling particularly exhausted, light-headed, undernourished, and rejected, I would head to a Catholic church on Oak Park Avenue when mass was not in session. With the sun shining through the stained-glass Jesus, I would go up front to one of the pews, get down on my knees, and pray toward the large, highly detailed cross on the wall straight ahead of me. "Dear God, help me."

I could not have been any further away from my playful and fun-loving self at Longfellow Park. The distance between me now and that little girl luxuriating in her body at Longfellow Park was like a spiritual crater.

I didn't know exactly what I should pray for as I kneeled there. Inside, I felt upside-down and my mind was like a scribble. Sergeant said, "You can't even sit up straight enough for the cross and Jesus. You want Jesus to know how terrible you really are?" You're a slacker! Slackers deserve to be punished!

I'd end up praying to lose more weight and to stay thin, and while doing that, I'd sit up straighter for Sergeant and, oh yes, Jesus.

I now believed that everything rode on my being thin enough. If I could just stay thin and do all my Sergeant drills right, my life would be good and I would be good enough . . . finally. Good enough that my dad might stop doing drugs, good enough that the yahoos would give me a pass into their club, good enough to have Sergeant let up on me, good enough to get my mom to spend less time at her job and be more available.

I believed **OCD math: Do X and you'll get Y.** By the way, because OCD is a tricky little bastard, X and Y were always changing variables. In this instance, X equaled "starve yourself and be perfect" and Y equaled "love and acceptance."

Without knowing it, I was a pawn in a big OCD game. Yep, it was the dance that Sergeant and I did. Do this to get that. No matter how outrageous it got, I still played. Sure, I would have liked to have gotten out, but like a battered wife and prisoner, I just didn't know how.

It sounds so strange to say it now, but I still didn't realize that Sergeant was nothing more than my raging OCD. What I would do to get those years back! I also had no idea that my eating disorder was what's called a "shadow syndrome" of OCD—a common problem suffered by many with OCD. I just thought this was the way I had to be and accepted it. I was terrified not to. I was terrified of Sergeant. I believed that he had the ability to make my hellish life even worse, and it was proven, he did. That is exactly what kept him in power and me a puppet. "You have to get thinner. Don't you see that is the only way for you to be successful?"

I'd stumble along from one drill to the next, catching fleeting moments of satisfaction and calm from having followed orders, but as quickly as those good and satisfying feelings would come, they'd go. Without having a clue, I was caught up in the OCD cycle from obsessions (horrible unwanted thoughts that cause anxiety) to compulsions (doing what

I had to do to get relief), and around and around we'd go. Sergeant was captivating. There was always more for me to do. He would change the games slightly, making them more challenging (levels within levels). This approach had my interest and even more holding power.

It's the same reason people can't stop playing Candy Crush Saga—there's always a new stage to unlock or level to beat.

—BEN PARR, *CAPTIVOLOGY*

Distracting Myself

On my sixteenth birthday (I can remember this because I was having a quiet moment by myself at the dining room table eating a piece of cold fried chicken), my brother Brian came in and said, "It's your birthday and we're going to get your license." Brian took me in his souped-up Impala, and we raced down Eisenhower Expressway to the Chicago driver's license facility. I'm fairly certain that the old guy who passed me on the driving test had never sat in a car with such a jacked-up ass, rust, and a bitchin' cassette player; it had teenage wheels written all over it. I was thankful to have my license but wished I could have finished that piece of cold fried chicken!

I found that driving did give me the sense of freedom that I longed for. I could leave and I could drive, and drive I did. It was empowering. I went everywhere, including the north side of Chicago, where there were loads of funky shops. I loved observing city life; it had a real mystique to me coming from the suburbs and all. Driving and going out drinking with friends gave me some desperately needed distractions from the litany of obsessions and compulsions. Then came my budding addictions, each one like a barnacle that gave me a little protection and my sensitive self some coverage, a little hiding place.

"Get Loose of the Noose!"

It was a weird purgatory. I was a bundle of anxiety and fixations and felt so much, but almost at the same time I felt nothing and was somewhat numb. Driving still offered a distraction, but at some point the car would have to park back home in its parking spot, and I would go back to being the fly in the bottle of white Elmer's glue. I was so deeply depressed that I really didn't know what to do with myself. I just dragged along, constantly trying to hit Sergeant's bull's-eye. In other words, I was trying to get loose of the noose. My efforts to satisfy Sergeant, at times, could bring temporary relief, but in the long run, just made the noose even tighter.

Therapy Time

My mom wasn't oblivious to the fact that things weren't right with me. During OCD fits, when I couldn't get my drills right or get myself feeling right with Sergeant yelling at me and what felt like continuously tapping on my shoulder without letup, I could be a real bitch to her.

Sometimes when my mom would say, "Kirsten, what is the matter with you?!" I would yell in her face, "What is the matter with *you*?!"

I was frequently demanding, redlined with anger, and annoyed at her. It's like everything that was bothering me would get pent up and then blast at her. I would tell her sternly, "I didn't ask to be here in the first place!"

I thought she should be held responsible. Finally, Mom took me to see a therapist, and I just burned up the hour. I darted and dodged getting to any real issues. It was my senior year, and by this time I weighed just ninety-eight pounds. The therapist told my mom privately that I "could have an eating disorder called anorexia nervosa" (you think?!) and that if I got down to ninety pounds that would be the time to worry, and I would probably need to go into the hospital. But until then I'd be fine, he said; just keep a look out.

I hated myself for being such a good actress while slowly killing myself. "Oh, I already ate," I'd say, or "I guess I just have a fast metabolism."

One time I was convinced that my digital scale was broken, and **EVERYTHING WAS RUINED!** I stomped around and cried and punched my thighs. All the while, I was less than a size zero. What I didn't know (and apparently neither did this therapist) was that I was experiencing body dysmorphic disorder, a body-image disorder characterized by persistent intrusive preoccupations with an imagined or slight defect in one's appearance.

DISREGARDED

CAN YOU SEE MY BROKEN BONES AND DEFORMITIES

POKING THROUGH MY HEAVY CLOAK HIDING MY MALFORMITIES

A VAPID SPIDER ONCE DESTROYED ME DEEP INSIDE MY BRAIN

WHEN I HIT MY TEENAGE YEARS I GREW IN KNOTS AND MAIMED

THE COVER-UP WAS ELABORATE TO DISTRACT FROM WHAT'S BENEATH

SELF-WORTH AT ZERO AND SOME MISSING TEETH

THE DEVIL PLUCKS AT WEAKNESS ALL THE PETALS TOSSED AWAY

WHEN YOUR SHINE IS STOLEN IN DARKNESS YOU MAY STAY

AS DARK AS ANY CORNER WERE EACH AND EVERY DAY

SO DEAD I FELT THE FLESH HUNG ON, TO SEE ME FADE AWAY

One day, about two years into my extreme dieting and weight loss, I opened the refrigerator at home and found a big, homemade heart-shaped cake slathered in white frosting with globs of red sugar sprinkles on it. It was clearly homemade by my brother's girlfriend for Valentine's Day. Without a moment's hesitation, I took the cake out of the fridge and, using only my hands, scooped the rich, extremely sweet white cake into my mouth, messy handful after messy handful. I almost choked it down, I was so starved. I ate almost the entire thing, leaving only a small piece of the left top curve of it.

When my brother saw what I'd done, he went ballistic on me. "What the hell is the matter with you? You are so fucking weird and unbelievable!"

Of course, there was also hell to pay with Sergeant. "You totally ruined your brother's surprise. He and his girlfriend think you're an asshole and you are! A fucking fat pig asshole. Today you will have very little to eat to pay for your inexcusable behavior!" I did as I was told.

For years afterward, I heard about my odd and unforgivable behavior from my brother and his girlfriend. Every time someone brought up the story again, I felt deeply ashamed and embarrassed. How could they not know how sick I was? Healthy people don't do that.

❖ ❖ ❖ ❖ ❖ ❖ ❖

My mom and I would talk about what we thought "I might have," what was plaguing me and not allowing me to rest, and why I had constant mental discomfort and an internal feeling of being shaken all the time. Worry could grab my ankle and drag me under. Sometimes I would have to leave class to go home and check

- the ashtrays for any still-burning cigarettes I may have carelessly left.

- the front door to make sure it was locked to prevent a bloodbath murder.

- the stove to make sure the burners weren't on to prevent a skin-melting fire.

- the faucets to make sure no water was running to prevent flooding and completely ruining all the things my mom had worked so hard for.

While my friends went away together on spring break, I stayed back. I couldn't let them find out how ill I really was and that I was only eating raw white mushrooms with mustard and store-bought cans of green beans. One night while all my friends were in Florida drinking rum runners, an angel came to me in a dream. She showed me versions of myself in cavern-like prison cells with no bars. The last one was shrieking and looked like a tormented ghost, flying wildly with no way out.

I woke up chanting, "I will forgive myself" again and again. At the time I didn't know how to interpret those words and their significance. But I did get the message of the dream: *Change your ways or you will die.* I started allowing myself to eat more, but I was not enjoying it. Finally, the school year ended and I graduated. It was a miracle.

Right after graduation, my main girlfriend, the one who had helped me plot and strategize through high school, and I went to Europe. So did Sergeant. While we were in Italy, I thought maybe I should take the train by myself to Sweden. Maybe there I'd find some happiness. But I was too mentally overwhelmed to deal with securing a ticket and all the details of navigating by myself. We returned to the US at the end of August.

Sergeant and I came back from Europe to a new living situation. My mom and her boyfriend of fifteen years, Richard, had gotten married. He had nine kids from a previous marriage, and my mom had us three. Out of everyone I was the youngest. Mom and Richard mainly waited for me to finish high school before signing the contract, but now the deed was done. Not only had they married, but they'd bought a new house, their dream home (he intended for them).

It was lovely. Perfectly perfect and spotless just like a model home. My mom was very proud of it. It had half-dollar-sized, peach-colored, rose-shaped guest soaps and peach-colored, velour, embroidered guest towels in the bathroom. Our lives before this had always been a little more scrappy. In her mind, she had arrived. In my mind, she had departed. *She and I* had departed. From each other.

Her new husband was demanding, highly opinionated, and prone to anger. Without question, he was the king of the castle. He had good traits—don't get me wrong. He was analytical, hardworking, smart, and a successful businessman. He had a green thumb, was a wonderful cook, and deeply loved his nine children, but it didn't take much for those good things to be overshadowed, especially living under his roof. He also had a tendency to redline when he perceived things weren't going his way. His rage was a lot like Sergeant's, and the two of them were just too much on my nervous system.

Richard would have preferred me out of the house completely so he and my mom could be alone and kid-free. I was messing with his dream, and believe me, I felt it. I was like the red wine spill on his white countertop. This feeling of being the odd girl out was wonderful kindling for Sergeant and brought me to another level of depression—not a step deeper into the dungeon, but a leap.

·3·

STORM OF A CHAOTIC MIND

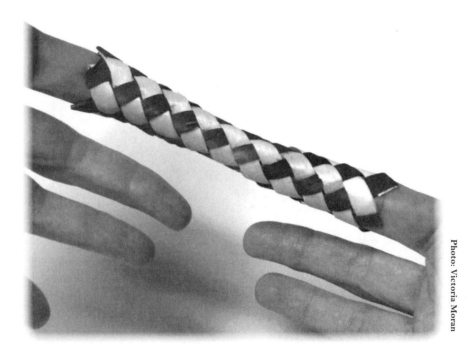

Congratulations, You've Arrived at Loser Land

Because my grades weren't so hot and I was lacking direction, I registered at the local community college, which a local DJ on a popular Chicago radio station had called a "high school with ashtrays." I felt like I was in Loser Land (or L.L.) big time and was *so* bummed about it; plus I had credit card debt from being in Europe all summer and completely mishandling my finances. I had to immediately get a shitty waitressing job to start paying off bills and get a shitty used car so I could *get to and from* all of this shittiness.

The first car of my own was a light loser-blue Toyota Celica. I bought it with no credit or money down from Cecil and Sammy's Used Car Lot. Of course, it broke down constantly. Just another domino in the domino effect of complete shittiness. That shit stacks up!

I'm not proud to say that I also started drinking and doing coke with strangers in dimly lit bars around town, like one called the Thirsty Whale. These strangers and I all had one thing in common: none of our lives were going right. The only things that made the bad, poorly mic'd '80s hair bands even close to tolerable were the drugs and the hope for more drugs coming. At the end of an evening, I would step out from behind the dark, heavy wooden doors into what was now ugly daylight. Let me tell you, it was grim and the day ahead was filled with no promise.

Temporarily, coke—cut with who knows what—would make me feel something, but then there was the other side of it, when the pony pack was licked clean, the coming down, and the ***head-first CRASH***. If Loser Land and my loserish jobs weren't enough to drive home me being a total loser, this sure was. *I just couldn't seem to step into the next right moment.* I was in total hate with myself and couldn't find my way out.

I hated college L.L. and partied late almost every night. The hangovers were wicked. My weight was heavier now, too, and I hated myself for getting a little chunky. I didn't dare get on the scale. I thought I would just die if I saw the number staring back at me in electronic red.

I still believed God was out there somewhere; I just didn't know where. I was convinced that my "real life" hadn't started yet, that this was all some kind of messed-up dress rehearsal. I was looking for my real life everywhere. I never imagined that it was under my two feet.

I wanted to be invisible. I started wearing layers on top of layers of clothing to cover my body. In the dead of summer, maybe three tops plus a windbreaker. My skin was so white from lack of sunlight it almost glowed.

I wasn't showering regularly because I was disgusted with my naked body and wanted to see as little of it as possible. When I was on my period, Sergeant would tell me that I was leaving bloody tampons everywhere. This was a new obsession. In fear, I would compulsively go back to the places that I had been and check just to make sure that there was nothing there. "There is no bloody tampon on the tile floor, Kirsten. There is no bloody tampon on the tile floor, Kirsten." I would say it out loud in hopes that it would sink into my thick skull so that I could move forward.

I was always wearing sunglasses, even while indoors. I would also wear my Sony Walkman everywhere, frequently with Peter Gabriel's "Red Rain" blasting in my ears. I didn't want to hear or see anything or anybody, and I wanted no reminders that I was there at L.L. with all the other kids who didn't make the cut.

Then the binge eating started. In the middle of the night, I would wake up and binge eat. The next day, I would always feel as guilty and as ashamed as shit. One time while my mom and the king were out, I ate almost two half-gallon tubs of his rich pecan-filled praline and caramel swirl ice cream in one sitting. I knew I couldn't leave the empty boxes for anyone to see. The king would have gone berserk. So I drove myself and the completely licked-out empty tubs to a nearby forest preserve and dumped them in the trash. I then drove to the grocery store, bought two identical tubs, and sat in the car trying to eat just the exact amounts out of each one so they looked just as he'd left them. Then I went home and stuck them back in the freezer, and by the time my mom and the king got back home, I had covered up another one of my crime scenes.

Every night for years, I got up and ate. With a lot of effort I could control myself during the day but had no control at night. At some point I tried securing myself to the bed with belts so I couldn't be so bad. That didn't work. My sleepy bad self would just take the belts off and quietly scrounge around the kitchen for something to devour. One time I ate all the chicken pieces out of Richard's chicken casserole and then mushed the noodles, carrots and peas back together. When Richard found out that I had done this, he yelled at my mother about what a "daughter she had."

And then there were the episodes of bulimic vomiting.

One night around this time, I ended the evening at Denny's and ran into one of the two boys from Mind Fuck University (aka high school). Not the one I turned myself inside out for but his bestie. My "sucker light" must have been on BIG TIME. With confidence in his gait, he walked right up to the booth where I was sitting and greeted me, evil delight in his twinkling eyes, "Oh, look at what we have here! **A failed anorexic!**" I was the moment's entertainment yet again. Although I was feeling like a victim, no fighting-back words came to me. I just felt really hurt and sort of froze in the booth.

Instead of saying "Fuck off!" as I should have, I said nothing and pulled his words in. Meanwhile, Sergeant grabbed the meanness and ran with it. Nothing had changed. Even after that boy had been such a shit to me over several years, I offered him a ride home and let him fuck me. I felt like dirt and that is what dirt does. He said, "Have a ten-pound bag of shit," and I said, "Make it twenty pounds."

Let It Snow

Smoking a cigarette was one way to get temporary relief. Smoking helped me check out. I'd get even deeper into my own head and deeper into my own noise, deeper into my own scribble and my own static. That's what the vacant smoking stare was all about—departure and cocooning.

I became a constant pleasure seeker. And an addict in the constant quest to find something that would make me feel good and take away some of the pain, including but not limited to Sergeant.

The biggest problem with my addiction was that, like all addictions, it sneaks up on you slowly. You give into it incrementally, in an almost imperceptible way.

—MIDDLE MEN

One addiction morphed into the next; in that respect, it had a similar nature to Sergeant.

The best place to get some cocaine was Austin Avenue. I spent a lot of time there scoring pony packs, an origami-type white paper triangle with the pure white powder dope inside. One night I went to score a pony pack at a different bar than the usual one (where my dealer stashed his coke behind the dartboard). When I walked into the new bar, I didn't know anyone. But I did know very quickly who was selling coke there. I am convinced that drug people share a wavelength. It's like we are tuned to the same channel. Channel W.D.R.U.G.S.

I scored some blow and did a line of it on the back of the toilet seat in the locked unisex bathroom. Once the high kicked in and my heart and head seemed to turn on, I walked out of the bathroom and felt a blunt object against my head. I turned to the right and looked straight into two barrels of a shotgun. Behind it was this crazy-eyed, unkempt old man I had never seen before. So what did I do? I put my hand up between my head and the barrels. I ducked down beneath the gun to get out of the crosshairs and just walked myself out of the bar. The imminent danger didn't rattle me one bit. In fact, it almost went unnoticed. I was just glad to have scored the cocaine.

On the same weekend, I went to a friend's sister's apartment to do some drugs. Her thing was PCP, or angel dust. She was a girl with a big heart and a messed-up mind. She never had much cash, so she would turn tricks with the dealer in her back bedroom, but I didn't care. Just as long as my coke held out. In the early morning, the dealer came staggering out of the bedroom and asked me for a ride, since I was the only one with a car. "Sure," I said. Why not? I was really good at killing time, and this seemed like an interesting thing to do. He said "That's cool, yo." I liked to drive fast and did exactly that on the Eisenhower Expressway heading east. As it turned out, I was taking him to a Chicago courthouse for his hearing.

While I was driving, he offered me a line of coke. I was glad that he had asked me, and I didn't have to ask him. This made me feel less like an addict. He tapped out a line, put a rolled dollar bill up to my nose, and with one big snort through my right nostril, bam, it was gone. I dropped him off. I never knew his name, and I never asked him why I was taking him to court or what he was busted for. It was just cooler to say, "Hey, good luck, man."

Drug addict math: Do X *drugs* and get Y *feeling better*. But the pockets of feeling better got smaller and smaller, and the leaps down into the dungeon got bigger and bigger. At this time I did think that God still saw me, but I just kept wandering aimlessly into the devil's palm and his long, grotesque fingernails were like my prison bars.

I must have had at least a half dozen odd jobs and waitressing jobs between the ages of nineteen and twenty-seven. My waitressing went all the way from greasy spoon, Greek-owned breakfast places, where my shift would start at 5 a.m. serving eggs and tossing toast to customers, to higher-end, white tablecloth Italian joints, where I poured loads of red wine and Dom Perignon until midnight or later.

One day at L.L. early on, the art teacher had us start bringing in our drawings and hanging them on the back wall for each other to critique. One guy's work really stood out, and it became a game for the rest of us to see who could spot which one was *his* first. This übertalented art guy's name was Doug. Just what he, with his truly developed talent, was doing in an introductory art class at this high school with ashtrays was way beyond me.

Doug sat in a row in front of me to the left. Every day in class he brought his big toolbox filled with well-organized art supplies, and he was always well dressed and had kind of a cool fashion thing going on. He sometimes had on light-colored chinos and a white cotton button-down shirt with a popular-of-the-times priest collar. He reminded me of the Professor from *Gilligan's Island*. Not a hair out of place, his shirt tucked in, and he always wore a belt. Sharp, smart, and about the only one who could be trusted in this community college's otherwise motley crew.

Most of the time, I felt as though I was hiding under a rock, trying to be in denial as much as possible about my present fate in L.L. However, the feeling I had around Doug was warmer, lighter, and brighter, and I even felt safe. My time with him was different. It didn't have the dark magnetic pull of so many of the other things in my life at that time.

Doug was also in my astronomy class, and one night during our long class break we were all standing in the hallway talking around a cement structure that was supposed to look like the moon (it didn't). I announced to the group that I had car trouble and asked if anyone could give me a ride home. Doug said, "I can." A classmate also on break said, "Jeez, dude, you don't even know where she lives."

On the drive, I told him that this was just a ride and it didn't mean I wanted to be his girlfriend. He said he knew that. When we arrived at the castle, I asked him if he wanted to come in for a glass of something like lemonade. He said, "Sure."

I wasn't sure why, but I took out my grandma's best vintage crystal to serve our glasses of lemonade. In fact, I was sort of irritated with myself that I didn't just give him a *regular glass* from the cabinet. We talked and talked, and we even laughed a bit about our mutual dislike for our crappy school.

I always looked forward to chatting with Doug. As if his general demeanor weren't enough of a giveaway, I discovered pretty quickly that his lifestyle was much different from mine. He woke up early on Saturday mornings to wash his car. Probably right around the time I'd be getting home from partying on the north side of Chicago. (One of those Saturdays, when I stopped at the corner gas station on my way home to pick up another pack of smokes around 5 a.m., I ran into my mom's husband, Richard, freshly showered and buying his morning paper. I think we acknowledged each other with a grunt. For us, that wasn't too bad; often that was as friendly as we got.)

Doug and I hung out more and more as "friends" as I faded in and out of relationships with other guys. I would often tell Doug that I wished my relationships with other guys were more like our relationship. "They just don't get me," I'd say.

Doug didn't know about Sergeant, of course, but Sergeant had plenty to say about Doug. "You know, Doug is too short for you. He's not even six feet tall, and he's like the Professor on *Gilligan's Island*—he's kind of a square. I think I might have seen him wearing a corduroy blazer with patches on the elbows. He doesn't do any drugs, so clearly he's out! And every Saturday morning while you're sleeping off another long night, he's up doing errands. He's really not for you."

Deep down, sadly, somewhere, I knew that a romantic relationship with Doug would never last. I knew that I couldn't stay well long enough. I thought the safest way to keep this guy in my life and not completely blow it was to just stay friends.

For years Doug wanted to be "more than friends" and I declined. The elaborate gifts that we gave each other at birthdays and holidays always made our current significant others quite irritated. We'd both say in retort, "What? We're just friends! God! They just don't get it."

The Zipper—1987:
Twenty-One Years Old

Artist: Doug Pagacz

Despite my unbridled anxieties, fears, and rituals, I used to seek out thrill rides. They reminded me that I was still alive and made me feel something past my layers of addictions and desperation.

My ride requirements: First, it needed to tap terror directly into my spinal column, to wow me out of my depression and soul numbness. Second, it had to be super high, at least a few stories up; and third, it had to be superfast, meaning all I would see was a blur of color as I whipped around violently, flipping and spinning. When I'd open my eyes for just a second, I might see only one thing in focus, like a car parked far away in the lot and everything else was a blur. Success! I loved the g-force pushing across my face hard, pressing into my cheeks and making them feel like they were wrapping around my ears. The more people screaming for their lives, the better. Let the adrenaline surge. (I had no idea that with OCD I had a monumental chemical imbalance, that my natural serotonin levels were off. It was like I was trying to turn myself on. Serotonin is the natural stuff that can help us feel good—mine wasn't working, clearly! Who knew?!)

The ride that met all of my criteria was the Zipper. POW! Like a shot to the arm, the Zipper would penetrate and shake my spinal column, making me feel *something*. This was my opportunity to Wake Up! Come To! Feel Alive!

It was powerful enough to get me out of my dreadful head and my uncomfortable body. If only for a couple of minutes, it made me feel **ALIVE**. It gave me that rush I was looking for that even cocaine couldn't do anymore.

I would beg and plead with Doug to go on the Zipper with me. If you aren't familiar with the Zipper, more power to you! I lived to catch a ride on this dangerous, surreal, whipping, and spine-crunching thing. (Now that I'm well, I am convinced that the Zipper was designed and created by someone who hates humans!)

Doug, good friend that he was, would come along, but he could not wait to be brought down again to street level, no Zipper. His thrill came when it was time to get out of our unsafe, rickety, barely locked metal cage. I could always convince him to ride it again, and only when my face had turned a nice pale shade of green would I feel like I'd had enough. Doug was always a trouper and was always way past that point by the time it was finally over.

Love of Retro

When not seeking out the Zipper, Doug and I always loved getting lost in an antique store. For me, it allowed Sergeant to chill a bit and my imagination to sail in a pleasant way. It was soothing. We both shared a passion for bygone eras and loved finding vintage gems. "I wonder who sat at this 1950s dinette set and used this Wonder Bread box? Were they a happy person or a sad person?" "Who's the woman that wore this Christmas corsage made of pink mesh and white plastic bells and silver foil leaves? Did she wear it just to church, or did she wear it everywhere? When did corsages go out of vogue, anyway?" Each item is a little time capsule with a different story. It felt like an honor to be looking at the pieces of someone's life.

I was in awe that things could survive so much time and human handling. It's as though they'd look up at me and say, "I'm still here!" Some items really spoke to me emotionally, and I would have this overwhelming desire to care for them and protect them. The collecting began.

Some of my all-time favorite things were the delicate vintage party favors that were still around. I was fascinated by the delicate colored paper, fluffy chenille, or thin and fragile celluloid. That they had not been crushed, ripped, destroyed, or thrown in the garbage was absolutely amazing.

Sometimes while in an antique store looking at items, I could feel the presence of the person who used to wear that ornate black onyx cat brooch or envision the lady who must have worn the caramel brown velvet pillbox hat with a striking dark green feather so perfectly placed, or I'd just stare at the patterns on the vintage men's ties with mid-century modern patterns, each carefully arranged on the spinning rack that I'd slowly twirl around.

I would take my continual cigarette breaks outside by myself. Sucking one down here and there so I could get back to brooding by myself in some deep thought.

❖   ❖   ❖   ❖   ❖   ❖   ❖

After three years, not two, I got out of L.L. with my associate's degree in liberal arts and so did Doug. He went on to the American Academy of Art, a prestigious art school in Chicago. I, on the other hand, started as a *junior* at Northern Illinois University in DeKalb. My mom paid for all of my tuition and my apartment rent. She was always generous, and I could have and should have been more thankful. I just couldn't seem to get past my own misery. One positive thing happened, though. I did decide to end my love affair with cocaine. Somewhere, somehow, I accessed the warrior within me, and she said, "Get out and stay out!"

At Northern, I isolated myself as much as I could and drank like a fish. I made some friends, had various boyfriends, but remained emotionally distant and mostly in my head with Sergeant. "Don't step on that sidewalk crack on the way to school, check your pants (not the ride) zipper, count sixteen times before that stranger passes you." So many rituals. If I didn't perform them, the anxiety that was associated with noncompliance was too much to bare.

I still attracted the dark side of life, and I was attracted to it as well. My invisible want ad must have read: *If you are depressed, schizophrenic, addicted, and make unhealthy decisions, if you project darkness instead of light, we will get along just fine!*

Sergeant commanded my attention and controlled the switch at my reward and punishment center in what seemed to be the deepest part of my brain. This was our relationship and it had been like this for more than ten years and going strong. He ominously talked right into the boom microphone inside my head. I knew not to talk about our private relationship. Telling on him and pissing him off terrified me. I would just follow his commands and orders. It was just easier this way. Otherwise, he would force-feed me obsessive thought after obsessive thought and my head would truly overload and it was not unlikely for me to break down crying.

I stopped standing up to him at all; I just didn't have the wherewithal to fight. I just complied because it was easier. I was checking, touching, tapping, blinking, calorie counting, doing and redoing, holding my breath, cleaning, staring, repeating, and ruminating (mentally going over and over something and not being able to stop myself). From one thing to the next to the next and loads of cigarettes in between.

Sergeant was the "what-if" master. "What if the stove was left on? What if your zipper is down and you're exposing yourself right now? Do you want a stranger to see your crotch, you careless whore?! What if you didn't lock the door? What if you lost your homework? What if your mom is going to just stop loving you?" These what ifs gave me a jolt of energy, a jolt of fear. Check! Check! Check! Check! I would check until the end of time if this would quiet Sergeant, if only for a little while. I needed my world to be right, and doing these things *right* still brought me moments of relief. It was all I felt I had to lean into to maintain some kind of sanity (if that sounds backward, it is!).

On several occasions I went back to the library to see if I could find out what I had. I would look up bipolar disorder or schizophrenia. I could relate to bits and pieces but not to all of the conditions. At this time *OCD* was not part of the common vernacular, and I still hadn't heard of it.

If you are getting the real sense that I was trapped, we are on the same page. It was strange. Doing the compulsions gave me a sense of control, but I was kidding myself: It was Sergeant who had the control.

You might be asking, "Just how is she going to get out from under Sergeant's 800-pound thumb? Just how is she going to get him out of her chaotic mind and find peace?" Right now, it all seems pretty damn hopeless, I know. However, I want you to know that I am living proof that hopelessness can turn into hopefulness and illness can turn into wellness. Just hang in there, and we'll get to much better parts, I promise. Keep the faith.

❖   ❖   ❖   ❖   ❖   ❖   ❖

I graduated from Northern Illinois with a bachelor's degree in communications and a minor in radio, TV, and film using only a small percentage of my brain that was still available and wasn't completely wrapped up with Sergeant. Those years mostly were a blur, or, better put, a smear. After graduation and in worse shape, I had no choice but to go back and live with my mom and her husband for a while.

I applied for a job at a limo company and was hired as a dispatcher. During training, I got stuck in some sort of mental glue like I had never experienced before. I was told that their fleet was for hire and that a lot of customers used their service to get to and from O'Hare Airport. When I mentioned that I had seen limos at O'Hare with signs in their front window saying NOT FOR HIRE, my trainer said those cars were probably part of their fleet. Now I was really confused. Why would they say "not for hire" if they were part of the fleet that was for hire? How could the fleet be for hire and not for hire at the same time? I kept having the trainer explain the *hire and not for hire* phenomenon to me, but I couldn't wrap my mind around it. I couldn't stop thinking about it. I couldn't stop obsessing about that mind riddle; it looped and looped and brought me to a new level of madness. Of course, Sergeant wouldn't do anything other than encourage more looping. I must have been quite the entertainment for Sergeant. He liked me just where he had me. He'd pester and pester me with that same question for fun with no letup.

My illness was devouring me, and the trainer at the limo place was not amused. He just looked at me like "What the hell is the matter with you?" I called and quit the next day.

I was too consumed by the riddle. For weeks, I played it over and over again in my head. That plus lack of sleep, poor nutrition, and my unhealthy lifestyle made for more great fuel for Sergeant. With a mind riddle, you need a complete answer, and often it is tougher to sit there and chew because ruminating (going over and over something in your head) is its own form of torture, its own form of spinning your mental wheels and getting hopelessly nowhere. Like tires spinning in deep mud.

A compulsion, although not the way out of OCD, at least gave me something to do about my nonstop obsessing. A physical compulsion gives you something to do in an attempt to feel better. Compulsions, though, more and more were bringing less and less of a reward, and I was feeling like there was no way out of me. I felt like I was walking backward in a forward-walking world. One riddle would fall back, and a new riddle would come forward. I was drowning in them and morbidly depressed (still having no idea that my natural serotonin levels were out of whack!).

Dancing Penguin

I was out of waitressing, and the first "real" job I got was at a cable company. I learned how to interview well, like an actor in a play. My job was to write and direct local cable commercials that would air on TV. I did like stretching my creative chops.

One day I got sent out to meet a new client, the business owner of a skating rink. I thought, *How cool is this? For my job I'm going to a skating rink.* As a kid, I had loved all kinds of skating—roller and ice. Skating was freeing. I kept my memories of these wholesome times tucked deep inside, where soul fossils reside, making our hearts feel fuller. My older adult self was expected to be on the surface now, clearly no room for fun; it was just too childish. In my early twenties, I was convinced that I was an adult and had to act that way, especially to be taken seriously by someone older.

At the rink I was greeted by a spindly older lady, who, it turned out, played organ for the skaters. She looked as if she'd dressed herself once in the 1970s and never took off her outfit. It was a light pink matching pantsuit with a small scarf tied in a knot around her neck. Her hair was frozen in time, too—a wispy bouffant that was high like cotton candy—and I could almost see through it. It had many layers of hairspray on it. In a sullen voice she said, "Follow me."

She took me to the room where they sold all the rink stuff to the kids. The room was dark, and the only things lit up were the glass fixtures in the back of the room and the owner's face. He was an intensely mean and odd man with a bad comb-over and thick black glasses. "You here for my commercial?" he grumbled. I hesitantly got closer to him so I could hear him better. He said, "I am going to be very specific with you, young lady. No niggers, no chinks! I only want good-looking white kids, and if you tell the local newspaper that I said any of this, I will deny it."

Did that just really happen? With my invisible hand, I did not let my mouth drop wide open. I am sure my eyes widened as I continued to take notes and then got out of there and away from his energy as quickly as I could.

On the day of the shoot, I told my cameraman, "Get B roll of everything, including *all colors of kids!* When the owner comes in for his video edit, I want our *greatest footage* to be of kids that aren't white."

On the day of the shoot, *among all kinds of kids* was a giant penguin. Like the kids, he was on skates, and he was waving and dancing around. Who was in the penguin suit? You guessed it. Mr. Happy Pants himself, probably with his sweaty comb-over glued to the inside top of the hollow penguin head. It felt like an alternate universe, similar to the one I was living in with Sergeant.

Here they were, Sergeant and this hateful man, but no one saw either of them. On the surface, my life was finally starting to look pretty good. Inside, it still felt anything but.

Pray for Neutral

I got involved with a new guy at this time. Our chemistry together was so strong that when we were near each other, the hair on our arms would stand up, literally. The high we got from being together was as addictive as any street drug. Sergeant even caught a contact buzz. It was as though we had found ourselves tucked into another dimension floating in a faraway space that had been put there just for us. The outside world was on pause; it seemed almost silly and unimportant.

The energy between us and around us changed and became a shade of dark that I had never seen before. Something was at play there that was bigger than the two of us. I wish I would have stopped looking for the off switch and just gotten out of the room.

We were sick together and for a long while equally sick apart. We each barely hobbled out with a cane.

Serial Killer

And then Sergeant convinced me that a serial killer was trying to hunt me down.

Sergeant informed me that the serial killer would see that *I do everything wrong*. The dewdrops that I left behind me would lead him right to me, and inevitably he would kill me. I became extremely paranoid, feeling as though everything I did was being monitored and harshly *JUDGED.*

**Quite an experience
to live in fear, isn't it?
That's what it is to be a slave.**

—*BLADE RUNNER* (MOVIE, 1982)

I remember one day parking my car in a regular-old-nothing-special-about-it-to-anyone-else parking space. But I fucked it all up. I didn't maneuver the car perfectly into the middle of the space, exactly between the white lines. I challenged myself to just leave it the way it was. For the first time in a long time, I triumphed. I didn't cave to the pressure of Sergeant's demands for perfection. I left my car right where it was, parked not perfectly straight, and headed into the municipal building where I had an errand to run.

Fear is like a pack of wild dogs down in the cellar.

—TARA BRACH, *RADICAL ACCEPTANCE*

I had to sign in at the front desk. *I WAS NOT TOTALLY PRESENT.* I was in an OCD trance and swept away in thought and obsessing. When I signed my name, my mind was still on the bad parking job, so my signature was not as good as I thought it should be. My healthy self urged, "Leave it! Don't rewrite it." My ill self screamed louder: "YOU are a FAILURE, leaving a trail for your serial killer to find you. How stupid can you be! First the car parked entirely wrong and now your pathetic signature! You're lazy!"

Fear is the anticipation of future pain.

—TARA BRACH, *RADICAL ACCEPTANCE*

Sick as I was, I was still aware enough to know that most people would have parked their car without really caring that it was not perfectly centered. They would also have signed their name in the book without thinking. *But other people's rules didn't apply to me. I felt like I had to be in the center of perfection, no slack cut.*

After all, I had a serial killer watching and tracking my every move and all because I was fucking things up all over the place. I would be punished and killed. Fear was Sergeant's weapon, and he knew just how to wield his tool against me.

Real Fear versus OCD Fear Can Be Perplexing

The lines between real danger and perceived OCD danger can be blurred. The OCDer's fear center is broken and misfiring. (I'm serious, it's a brain thing! It's like we have a car alarm that is broken and keeps going off. So we are feeling fear just about all the time—fear about what will happen, what could happen, what might happen—however, our gatekeeper is OCD, and he is full of shit.)

Okay, so real fear and OCD fear are both hardwired into the brain. How do you possibly sort out the "real stuff" from the "OCD stuff" when *it all seems and feels equally real*? The topic of fear is one of the trickiest parts about OCD, and becoming acutely aware of real fear versus OCD fear takes a lot of work and practice (especially when they both truly do feel the same to the OCD sufferer). We will talk more about this later in the book.

Larva

I learned this lesson intimately about the universe in some of my darkest days: when you are terrified, which I was from second to second, people with bad intentions can sense your fear; you're like a wounded animal and they can smell it and prey on it.

Televangelists get viewers to send in money because the viewers are terrified of going to hell. Televangelists promise them a way to get to heaven. With their mesmerizing gaze, they hypnotize viewers to open up their wallets. By the same token, sadists, those people who get off on your pain, can, through fear, find their way in for a soul munch.

One day I took my cat Cleo to a new vet. He wanted to talk with me about cat stool. He went on and on for fifteen minutes about cat stool. His technique was like that of a drill, and his energy and eyes were weird and threw me off-balance. At one point, he looked right into my eyes as though my innate terror was delicious to him. He said quietly as he leaned into my personal space with intent, "In the cat stool, it's important to look for white things that look like rice." Then he unexpectedly raised his voice. "They could be *LARVA*!" He knew exactly what he was doing, scaring me, and he found my fear satisfying. Was he a psychic vampire? I believe to this day the answer is a resounding *YES*! However, Sergeant, my undiagnosed OCD, amplified my experience like it so frequently did.

Please Repeat That Please Repeat That

Once when I felt the world positively closing in on me and couldn't take it anymore, I asked my mom if she would treat me to a night's stay in a hotel room in nearby Bolingbrook, Illinois. I thought if I could just get some solid rest, I'd maybe snap out of this craziness. She did treat me to a one-night stay, but of course my mind came with me (that seemed to be the never-ending problem). I had a restless night and felt trapped the whole time. The next day she met me there, and we wandered around a little bit and came across an empty banquet hall. We snuck onto the dance floor, and I asked her if she'd dance with me. "Mom, let's pretend we're butterflies, floating freely at a butterfly ball." We did. More glimmers of heaven, this time without the dark underside. Then back to business as usual.

About a day later, I called my mom and asked her to come over. At the time I was living with a lady, I had worked with at the cable company, Joan.

Hearing the stress in my voice, Mom came by. We lay on my bed, and I showed her my extensive notebook filled with the names of all the men who might kill me. I had been taking notes for several months, and I had compiled a list of about thirty men who I seriously thought might come and murder me, my ex at the top of this list. I wanted her to have the list so when something happened, she would know where and whom to investigate.

I asked her to repeat comforting words over and over for me just a certain way. "I will give the list to the authorities. I will give the list to the authorities, Honey."

"Mom, say it perfectly like you really mean it and don't say it with the word *Honey* at the end; that's wrong!" Although reassurance that she thought I wouldn't get murdered and her word repetition temporarily relieved my anxieties, my comfort was only fleeting. How I just wanted to hold on to it.

Leap of Faith

As strange as this might sound, a human angel dropped in on all this scribble. His name was Bernie. He was like a spiritual teacher. I met him while I was working for a short period of time doing light office work for a small jobs contractor. Bernie was a carpet and tile sales-man, and he also volunteered with recovering addicts and runaways. I told him that one day I wanted to help people, too. He said something like this, "You know when you're on an airplane and you're watching their instruction video about what to do in the case of an emergency? The parent gives the oxygen to themselves first before giving it to their kid." I saw what he was saying yet had no idea how to get there.

He and I struck up a friendship, and he started talking with me about *energy*. He said my energy was like a buzz saw, and my vibration was very low. I needed redirection and transformation. He turned me on to the books *Way of the Peaceful Warrior* and *No Ordinary Moments* by Dan Millman (treasures to this day). These books opened my eyes to the possibility of a different, more positive landscape, a brightness and lightness from which I felt very far away at that time.

On one of our mentoring adventures, Bernie and I went to a forest preserve. First, he brought me down a pretty challenging path strewn with thorny branches. The area around us was dark, heavily shaded, and cold; the mud was squishy; there were tree stumps and deadness. It all felt like immobility. A very familiar feeling to me.

After we were there for about twenty minutes or so, he led me out and had me follow him to another part of the forest.

Here, the sun was shining; there were butterflies everywhere, flitting around and gently landing on hundreds of knee-high white wildflowers.

This place felt like love and openness, and I could actually feel little sparks of joy inside myself. Wow, it had been a while since I'd felt like that.

We just stood there and breathed it in.

When we got back to Bernie's car, we paused for a few more moments and looked back at the forest preserve from a distance. He asked me what I saw in front of me.

I said, "I see the forest."

Then he asked me what I had learned.

I sat there quietly for a few minutes and then said, "The forest is like life itself; there is real darkness and there is real light. It's all there. It's all there all the time."

Find your inner plug. See what it is plugged into. Unplug. Replug into the strength, love and the power from God.

—JOHN EDWARD, *INFINITE QUEST*

"You gotta do the dance, Kirsten," Bernie said, handing me one of his imported cigars to smoke on our drive back. This cigar was a gift, his way of letting me know that I'd been a good student that day.

The last time I saw him we met on a Sunday morning at a break-fast shop. He asked me, "What do you need to do next, Kirsten?" I told him that I needed to make a "leap of faith." I wasn't even completely sure what I meant when I said it. But he smiled at me and seemed to like my answer.

When I met Bernie, I was spiritually out of tune. I felt like a de-pleted and empty vessel. I made a conscious choice after the last time I saw him to reset my internal compass. I had a long way to go on my spiritual journey (even outside of OCD), but I was determined to get to a better place.

I wrote "Sick Pond" about 15 years later, and wanted to include it in the book.

SICK POND

THREE-EYED SQUIRMIES LIVE
IN PEA GREEN GOO.
LITTLE FISH WITH SHARP TEETH.
FROG-LIKE CREATURES NEVER MOVE,
LEGS BROKEN.
HOT BUBBLES ON THE SURFACE
OF SOMETHING DEAD.
SICK HERE. SICK POND.
TREE BARK GUMMY AND THE SKY GRAY.
SCREAMS ECHO THROUGH THE SPINY BUSHES,
AIR CHILLY AND DEAD.
HAPPINESS ABSENT, GIRLS WITH BROKEN DOLLS
SIT UNDER SCARY-FACED TREES.
I HAVE BEEN HERE
BUT NOW I REFUSE TO GO.

With more clarity than I had experienced in a very long time, I drove directly to Doug's. I hadn't seen Doug for about a year and a half, having broken off our friendship when my intense relationship wouldn't allow it. I knew that he might not even speak with me.

Doug was living in an apartment built around the 1940s in Riverside, Illinois. I rang the deep, old-sounding buzzer and stood there at the bottom of the large, dark wooden staircase with my heart pounding, holding back tears, feeling so raw and exposed. Sergeant even stepped aside for this. This was the closest that I had ever come to truth. I felt as though I was standing in the middle of it.

I could see Doug coming down the stairs and said quickly to him, "If you give me a chance to be your friend again, I will never leave. I am sorry for being such an asshole." He gave me a slight smile and asked if I wanted to come up to his apartment. The second my foot hit the first stair, I felt I was on the right path.

Drive Radical Sabbatical — 1993

Almost immediately Doug and I quit our respective jobs, stayed broken up with our previous partners, and headed west. This was long before Google or GPS, of course, and we charted our course on a map. We drove from Chicago out to California on what was still left of old Route 66.

I took the opportunity of the new beginning to quit smoking, and I'd sit there in the passenger seat like a wild, seat-belted bunny, battling fierce nicotine withdrawal while swilling caffe lattes and devouring bag after bag of baby carrots. Old habits do die hard. But I wanted to start being healthier like Doug. I quickly, however, replaced the nicotine with caffeine.

The long car ride gave Doug and me a chance to catch up on everything that had been happening in our lives. Not to my surprise, his was fairly intact and he seemed quite healthy. His stability was intriguing to me.

I told him that there was something blocking my essence. Like barnacles that have been covering a rock for years, spiritually, mentally, physically, and emotionally. I told him that there was something else troubling me deeply. I was unable to sit still; I was unable to be quiet in my own head for any time at all. I was unable to rest, and it was exhausting.

With hours to talk, Doug and I tried to get in there and figure out what was going on with me. We probed around in the darkness with a flashlight. We talked and talked as we searched for the piece that would not let me experience peace. The part of my mind and spirit that felt broken.

I told him that I felt there was a monster, a "something" behind the curtain. We tried to find all the Oogie Boogie men hiding in the corners of my mind.

Questions came up: What was driving my fear? What was making me clean the refrigerator and toaster over and over again religiously? What was making me so worried that all the pictures in my house weren't hung straight enough? What was making me think that I'd left the oven or stove on every time I left the house? Why did I have to do the cord checks? What was making me feel like I was always leaving the door unlocked?

We talked about my dad and some of my crazy experiences with him. We talked about my eating disorder. We talked about the lack of consistent guidance and stability I had had growing up. We thought and thought some more. Something was there in the shadows. Something like a monster hiding in the corner, not wanting to be seen by the light.

What was bothering me so? We would shine a light inside the dark tunnel of my being, and he *(what felt like a wild monkey)* would jump to the next dark corner. Something was there, something was wild, and it was something we had never seen before, something that had control, and something that was leading my life. I caught glimpses of the outside edges of his wild hair, but that was all.

I had no idea at that point that this creature was a new manifestation of Sergeant. In fact, Sergeant himself didn't even have a name yet. I gave him a name only when I started writing this book. And now he'd taken on this new form. As we talked about this wild monkey presence inside me, I tried to describe how he would completely take over my thinking, even my every breath at times. Little did we know that we were starting the long expedition of discovery, *the big reveal* that would end up changing my, and our, life.

Many weeks and states later, we got back to Chicago. Doug broke up with me—or whatever it was we were doing. He said, "I can't do this with you right now." What did I do immediately? What did I do to cope? What I had done since I was thirteen years old. I went straight out and bought a pack of cigarettes, of course! Then I drove over to see the ex-boyfriend. What I realize now is that my unhealthy self was bringing me back to dive in. It's as though there was a ragged edge that was left there, and I wanted to fix it yet again.

I saw my ex-boyfriend's car outside and knew he was in his apartment. I knocked and knocked. He didn't come to the door. Finally, I left. Later, I heard from a mutual friend that he was lying on his bed, which was on the floor—similar to my dad's—with pillows over his head and ears trying to drown out my knocking, and that not answering that door was the hardest thing he had ever done in his life. I always thought I was the one who pulled the final trigger on the relationship and blew it up to oblivion, but it was him. By not coming to the door, he saved us.

After we'd been back about a week, Doug called and asked me if I wanted to go to his aunt's house for the Fourth of July holiday. "She has a pontoon boat that we could go out on." "Nope," I said and hung up quite listlessly. He called me again after the fourth and said it was a very lonely, sucky day for him. He asked to see me and I agreed.

Doug told me later that he didn't have "clearance to land" in our relationship. He said that he felt like he still had fall leaves on him from his previous relationship. That he couldn't jump in the pool if he still had leaves on him. We took a brief time out and then rerouted back to each other.

Lilac Village

A couple of months passed, and Doug and I got a small apartment in Lombard, Illinois. When the lilacs were in bloom, the air smelled magnificent, like the best perfume you could imagine. By this time, I was working in the marketing department at a crafting magazine.

In hopes of finding a better and more creative gig, I did some research at the public library. (Yep, that's how we used to do it, pre-Internet, LinkedIn, social media, etc.) While hunting around, I found a magazine article about a kid's educational toy company in the Bay Area of California. The article was all about the inspirational and bright female owner who started the company. I felt as though I had to meet her. And I liked that the products were educational and for kids. I was certain she'd have a marketing department and a place for me.

Was the "wild animal" still there hiding in the corners of my mind? Was I still doing bizarre rituals? You betcha! I was living a double life— one where I was a gal in her twenties trying to form a successful career path and one where I was still on Sergeant's whipping post. I was still having trouble getting from one moment to the next; I felt very little peace. The most peace I got to feel was sharing time with Doug. One thing I can say about my intensive boot camp with Sergeant: I had developed the ability to laser focus and work very hard toward any goal set before me. I could hunker down like nobody's business. My new quest was to get Doug's and my ass to California and start working for this company. *How to get my face in front of the owner?*

I decided to send a large package of my work samples directly to her. I took the video reels I was most proud of from the cable production job, put them and my résumé into a clean, empty gallon paint can, and created a fun label listing some of the things I could offer her and her company. Then, as a final touch, I wrapped the large outer box in white butcher paper and splattered it with colorful paint splotches. I figured she'd have to at least take notice of my creative energy.

I guess she liked it! I was flown out to California to have a meeting with the mystery lady at the famous and beautiful Hotel del Coronado in San Diego, right on the beach.

When I arrived, one of the company's well-put-together, size 2, well-dressed executives met me and took me to *her* suite. I was told in the elevator that the toy company owner would be very casually dressed, with no makeup and very casual clothes on. "She is resting for a big sales event tonight." The door opened to this marvelous and sprawling suite with an ocean view; there was even a giant and bountiful fruit basket on the table. It looked like this lady had it made.

Was I on the set of a James Bond movie or what?! In my head I said to myself, "Be here now! Be here now!"

I waited on the couch in the living room for the owner to appear. The idle time of waiting for her started to rev up my anxiety (Sergeant knew how to unleash all kinds of ruckus during idle time. Idle time was Sergeant's time to thrive!) I remember saying, "Kirsten, keep your shit together. This is major leagues; keep your shit together."

The owner greeted me with a lovely smile and looked directly into my eyes as she shook my hand. We talked about her company, how it had started out in her garage, and the various things she was doing today with her sales and marketing team to keep sales growing. I was very impressed with all that she had accomplished. What a woman! I think we took to one another, partially because we liked the fact that the other was creative with an undeniably independent spirit.

I got the job! Doug and I were moving to California with my cat Cleo—who, by the way, never did get **LARVA** in her stool! Thanks, freaky doctor, for that!

Here's Where OCD Can Get Dicey (It Gets Dicey Everywhere but Here's a Biggie)

Before hiring me, the company laid off a considerable number of their staff to cut costs (I had no idea). So the team that I was sent to work with had just seen some of their close friends lose their jobs. They were a disgruntled group and a very tight clique.

When I arrived on day one, I was escorted to a work area about half the size of everyone else's. I was put up against a wall and welcomed with a dusty old desk and an ancient computer. The beginning of the hazing had begun, and it sucked. The hazing turned into lack of general acceptance, and it went on for years. I didn't have the skill set at this time to make things any better.

But Here's the OCD Snageroo

I had low self-esteem tapes playing in my head lots and lots of the time, and I still had the constant feeling of someone tapping on my shoulder and not letting up, à la Sergeant. Plus OCD is the great amplifier. So the very real and painful things that my new colleagues did—like not accept me, not share information with me, not include me in lunches, etc.—got jacked way up in my brain. Sergeant would frequently shout, "**THEY HATE YOU!**"

How I wish I could have said, "Hey! You guys are being assholes. Cut it out." Instead, I just got quiet and got injured. At home by myself, I'd tug forcefully on my bangs and cry if I felt that they looked or felt uneven. Frequently, I would resort to cutting them myself to make them shorter and straighter across my forehead. Doug would ask me to just leave them alone. Somehow they gave me something tangible that I could unleash my angst on.

By now, I had thousands of anxiety triggers and anxiety responses. It was a lot like the game called Operation I fondly remembered from the

1970s. Remember what would happen when your metal tool touched the wrong metal area, and you'd get that zap? For us OCDers, we have thousands and thousands of chances of getting zapped every day (it's tough on the nervous system and **we do everything to navigate and avoid getting zapped constantly. We work within a certain confined space that Sergeant lays out for us).** The zapping and constriction—that has a lot to do with why we feel so stressed out and frazzled and often seem so short-tempered and rigid.

Here's a picture of my *fried-out* self at a convention for work. I had been at the toy company for a couple of years by then. I didn't like things touching me, really. Check out how big this suit is on me, my crazy eyes, and the very deliberately cut bangs. I was so deep in my acrylic box and trapped. My brain had two tracks: one the functioning and excelling employee and the other my own full-time radio station called W.O.C.D. They both ran at the same time.

Meanwhile, my performance reviews were always stellar. One boss was impressed with my thoroughness and drive. I guess I have Sergeant to thank (?) for that.

The Pusher and the Puller

One day I was walking down the hallway at work and ended up next to a set of floor-to-ceiling glass doors. The head of the printing department happened to be there at the same time. We were both headed in the same direction. Beautiful and tough, she was a pilot, wore miniskirts, had great long legs, and talked like a trucker. She never went to the washroom; she made "pit stops."

With the two glass doors in front of us, she said, "I love to watch what people do here. In life there are pushers and pullers." She grabbed the chrome handle and pushed it like a football player pushing through a line of guys. I had the chrome handle of the other door in my hand. As she pushed her way through, I was pulling my door lethargically toward me. It felt very passive and weak, with no gusto. *Fuck!* I thought to myself. *I'm a puller! I want to be a pusher like her!*

Kindness . . . a Lap of Cream for the Soul

One of the hardest things for someone with OCD is letting go—knowing when enough's enough. I leaned on Sergeant for this direction. I had written a couple of pages outlining a marketing promotion for the company's sales team. It was just about to go to press and become permanent, and I was stuck in mental glue **AGAIN**. I must have read and reread that thing a hundred times to make certain that it was perfect without any mistakes. When I gave it to a team manager, I was so nervous. I said, "I really tried to make this perfect, without any errors." She looked at me with understanding, accepting, and wise blue eyes like she knew something. Maybe she knew that I was scared.

She went on to say something like this to me: "There's a story in my husband's religion. It pertains to the making of ornate, handmade Persian woven rugs. The weavers try to make the rugs as flawless as possible; it is a painstaking effort. However, once the rug is finished and reviewed, if they see no flaw in the rug, then they turn the rug to its back side and intentionally make a small flaw of some kind. She said that the purpose of this is to remind themselves that *God is the only one able to make perfection.* This is their way of serving God and remaining humble. To do otherwise would be disloyal."

She had just given me the best gift. *Just the idea* of retiring from perfectionism was uplifting. She gave me a little window into another reality.

Eat Some Ice Cream and Have Some Fun

At this time, I was experiencing extreme tightness in my shoulders and back, so I went to a chiropractor. He was a groovy doctor with long, flowing hair, and he seemed very centered and with it. He asked how things were going, and I confided in him that I was terribly stressed and anxious at work. My uptight vibe was probably apparent. He worked on my back, and before I left his office he suggested this: "Eat some ice cream and have some fun."

Most folks would find that to be very good advice. Simple and doable. I just felt more sad knowing how damn far I was from *just eating some ice cream and having some fun.*

BUILDING TOWARD A CRESCENDO

Yoga and the Killing Bible

round the same time I thought I'd give yoga a try. I signed up for a class.

I was able to sit with my legs crossed and my eyes closed for about ten seconds. I couldn't be in my head a second longer. Mind you, the yoga teacher was so beautiful sitting up in front of everyone like a goddess. She radiated wisdom in her neutral and flowy outfit with her long, glistening white hair. All I could think was, *I have got to get the fuck out of here!*

I tried to act like I just remembered something that I had to go do. I tried to exit with my whole body saying, "Gosh, so sorry. I will try to quietly move my ass and get out of here quickly." I caught the eye of the teacher and flashed a crooked smile with a slight head tilt, trying to say "sorry" with all of my face. It was hard to be invisible in the black and bright green spandex that I chose to wear. I had to be careful not to step on everyone else's restful hands gently planted on their yoga mats. Of course, the wooden floor creaked obnoxiously as I extricated my absolutely-no-ability-to-do-yoga self.

Then there was the Killing Bible. I was obsessed more than ever with organizing. I had bought a new address book (remember, this was way before smartphones) and had had it for about one week, unable to use it. The very thought of it loomed heavily in my mind. I saw it as imperfect (I don't even remember why). So I drove to the mall and returned it.

But as I drove away, I became fixated on the idea that I had left it completely filled with names, addresses, and phone numbers. I was experiencing Thought Action Fusion, where the lines between reality and OCD reality are completely blurred and incredibly confusing. Sometimes people with OCD are misdiagnosed because of Thought Action Fusion. Not having a grasp or reality of what really did or didn't happen can sound like schizophrenia.

I knew that whoever found my address book next would use it as a Killing Bible and that I had laid it all out for them! I was in my OCD trance. I went back to the store to retrieve the Killing Bible and never was able to locate it. It was gone. For months I would see that damn maroon book floating in front of my face. That, combined with the procession of terrifying visuals of people being stabbed streaming through my head, was exhausting. I couldn't find the off switch and how desperately I wanted to.

1997: Thirty-One Years Old
My List of Can't Dos
(Just the Ones I Can Remember)

- I can't have certain things touch or confine me. I wear shoes that are size 9.5 or 10 when my feet are actually a size 8 so the shoes won't fully touch my feet.

- I can't touch newspaper. The dryness and chalkiness of the paper feel too horrible on my hands, as if its residue could never be completely rinsed off. After touching newspaper, I become highly distracted and agitated and can't stop thinking about my hands.

- I can't eat a meal without writing down all the calories and reviewing my intake over and over again.

- I can't use certain pens. They are unlucky pens, and if I use one of them, I'll bring bad luck to me and to the people that I love.

- I can't go without checking my purse every fifteen minutes. I open it, dig around, touch and look at everything in it, and reorganize the contents. I memorize the contents and the placement of every item . . . checkbook, hairbrush, lipstick, pen, sharpened pencil, tissue, cash in wallet, car keys! I mentally quiz myself several times over and over again. Zip it back up. Set it beside me. Do it again in fifteen minutes. If I don't do this, Sergeant will play a mental movie for me. This time, it's my mom dying in a car crash; it's a hit-and-run and no one sees the perpetrator's face.

- I can't write notes on small pieces of paper out of fear that I will write something defamatory, leave it behind, and subsequently be killed for it. I frequently imagine that I have written notes even when I have not.

- I can't leave answering machine messages without severe anxiety. I listen to them over and over again, making sure I did not say something defamatory or screw something up on the recording. I feel as though I have to leave the perfect message, with the right pronunciation and tone.

- I can't hear most things just once. Frequently, I have to have people repeat their sentences. I fear that if I don't hear all of the words right and get their intended meaning someone will die.

- I can't wear certain fabrics. Absolutely nothing itchy or confining; otherwise, I cannot concentrate on anything other than the terrible feeling on my skin.

- I can't have my tongue just resting in my mouth most times. My tongue has to touch the back of my teeth in a certain way a certain number of times. Sometimes Sergeant will say, "Have your tongue tap the back of your front teeth three times." Sometimes forty-two times. Sometimes Sergeant changes the number midway through just to screw me up. Sometimes I have to do this and tap my finger at the same time. It's unnerving. Sometimes I have to do this when I am supposed to be listening to someone right in front of me.

- I can't leave my house without having perfectly straight electrical cords. *All* electrical cords *exactly* and fucking precisely straight.

- I can't stop recording the names of the people that I have met who might kill me. I review this list of potential killers with my mom over and over again, so that when I die, she will be familiar with the list and will know whom to investigate with the police.

- I can't leave my house without checking the burners on the stove over and over again, sometimes up to one hundred times if not more. If I don't do this important check, I believe the house will burn down. Sometimes I leave the house and then have to come back to recheck.

- I can't just *go eat ice cream and have some fun* like my chiropractor suggested. That activity is for normal people and way too far out of my reach.

Oh, and just like always, I had to do all these things with no one noticing. I couldn't expose my private world, or I would be murdered. It was all a secret; otherwise, **D-E-A-T-H!** I would do anything to avoid death, and Sergeant's broad, unforgiving shoulders knew this.

Still my every action and thought put dew on the web as I tried to move forward. Every piece of food chewed incorrectly, another drop of dew; every action, another drop of dew. My world was closing in on me. I knew my serial killer would see my dewdrops and know exactly where I had been, what I had done, what I had thought. He would see that I do everything wrong and that I am a total unforgivable fuckup. My careless trail would lead him right to me.

I was checking, touching, tapping, blinking, calorie counting, ruminating, doing and redoing, holding my breath, cleaning, staring, repeating. I needed my world to be right, and I didn't know what else I could do. I had been reporting to Sergeant for twenty-plus years by now (privately). Some deep grooves of just how I needed to be were ingrained in my being.

If I could get myself to lift the record needle out of the groove and drop it somewhere else, I would. However, it was only a short amount of time before the next groove, before I would drop into my illness again. Trapped? Fuck yes! My OCD moments had become so frequent that they were now nearly constant. I had no more normal space left. I was trying to control everything so I wouldn't just bust apart at the seams. My world was getting smaller as I tried to not get zapped.

LITTLE MISS PARTICULAR

Little Miss Particular has to have things her way
If everything is not right
She'll have a horrid day
Things must be done like this
Not like that or not like this
Everything is measured to a tee
There are colors, flavors, and music,
Not let in you see
If she gets something that she does not like
A big old fuss is made,
You have to make adjustments
and they have to be this way
Her Judge and Jury are always out
I guess she's just the girl without

I was tightly gripping on to a handful of sand and it was just pouring through my fingers.

Bright Pink Piece of Paper

FEAR = False Evidence Appearing Real.

More OCD math: X = You have written something bad; you have to go get it. Or Y = You will be killed. I believed it.

By this point, I had totally bought into the program. I was twenty-one years into undiagnosed OCD. Sergeant was my Jim Jones, and I drank the Kool-Aid whenever he said, "Take a sip, bitch."

The toy company where I worked was in the Bay Area, about forty-five minutes east of San Francisco. There were rolling hills, magenta flowering bushes, and mountains everywhere. It was picturesque. On my drive home one night, I remember taking a moment to feel so fortunate to have this great relatively new job and to be living in the Bay Area with Doug.

Suddenly, as I was having a moment of appreciation and calm, the looming Sergeant spoke. I instantly felt unbridled anxiety. He said in his direct and unavoidable tone, "Did you see that bright piece of pink paper you just passed on the hill?"

I did see that bright piece of pink paper on the hill! The bright pink paper was clinging in the wind to the metal fence I had just passed.

"You have to get it! It has defamatory things written on it that you wrote about your office colleagues. That was so stupid of you, and it will get you fired if anyone were to see it!" I started to obsess that I had written horrible things on it, and I would be punished as the outcome.

With the paper being bright pink and only a minute away from the office, I knew the wrong person would get their hands on it. "Once they have this paper, you are done for." My heart pounded, my anxiety rose, and my vision started to blur. "You have to go back and get it, fool!" I knew that I had no other choice but to turn the car around and get the incriminating evidence. The evidence that would prove I am a bad person. This was the evidence that would end my career, sending Doug and me back to Chicago. Back to forcing my creative thoughts into yellow page ads, and it would all be my fault.

As soon as I could, I turned the car around and drove close to the pink paper. I parked headed dangerously down a steep hill. There I was, wearing my new work skirt, blazer, and heels, and running to the fence to get the evidence that said how I hated everyone. The evidence that said, "You are all motherfuckers," with my stupid signature! People from the office might see me. It didn't matter; I knew that I would make up some story later as to why I was there, like I always did. I remember my heels pressing into the grass and mud as I tried to move quickly to reach the paper, scaling the fence near the highway.

Finally, I got it! I took off my heels and ran as fast as I could to the car. Sergeant said, "Don't look at it. Drive away before anyone sees you!" That's exactly what I did. I knew I had to get rid of the evidence, so I ripped the paper up into little pieces, which I then soaked in my water bottle. The water smeared the ink, so it could never be read.

So much for the nice drive home, for the mountains and the flowers! I drove fast, knowing that I had done the right thing and that this time I was saved. This time I was spared.

I followed Sergeant's orders. I never even looked at the paper.

China Cups Crash

As if everything I've written so far isn't evidence enough of my complete unraveling, there was this:

Walnut Creek is a bustling town in the San Francisco Bay Area. It's much more urban and trendy than nearby Benicia, where we live. There is a Crate & Barrel, a Pottery Barn, an Apple store, and several coffee shops, including more than one Starbucks.

On this particular morning, the air was crisp and clean, and the sunshine was bright. I had my sunglasses on. This was a great day to wear them.

I was trying out a new posh hair salon that I had never been to before. My hair, dark auburn at the time, was in a chin-length bob, and the severe angle of it and my bangs needed an excellent trim to bring it back to the perfection bull's-eye. My new hairstylist was a tall, slender man. I was tense in his chair. My shoulders were tight, and my mind was jumping all over the place.

I sat there scanning the salon vigilantly, taking in all the visual cues and the vibe of the modern shop. The stylist and I chatted a little, but I was not able to tune in to our conversation at all. It was probably the haircut usual: "What are you doing this weekend? Do you have any kids?" I likely gave short answers. The shallow questions and answers that continued to pop up led to more feelings of isolation, of coming up empty like a deep echo between us.

When he was through cutting my hair, it was time to pay. I rummaged in my bag for my checkbook, forestalling the inevitable.

A check involves paper and a pen, both items that I struggle with terribly. Whenever I hold paper and pen in my hands, and sometimes even when I don't, I obsess that I have written shocking, malicious, and hurtful things—and signed my name and left it there in the open for everyone to see.

I wrote the check and handed it to the guy, but I was immediately gripped with fear. *What if I'd written "Fuck You, You Gay Bastard Hairstylist Fuck!"on that check? I did. I did write that. Why was I stupid enough to do that? Where is the door to get me out of this room? Oh my God, how am I going to get out?*

I could hardly breathe; I couldn't feel air getting into my lungs. I was trying to look normal with my shaky, crooked smile, but I could feel full body and mind paralysis take over. A shot of pure stress ripped through my body and straight into my head. My head was pounding.

Meanwhile, Doug was outside waiting for me on the sidewalk in front of the salon, undoubtedly enjoying the beautiful day. He'd been looking forward to our upcoming drive to Mountain View to visit some good friends that he met in art school in Chicago and had stayed in touch with.

Doug saw me, then smiled, and said, "Your hair looks good; do you like it?" I shrugged my shoulders and tried to nod yes as my world was still spinning. Holding back the tears and stress was like trying to hold back the ocean with only one wooden two-by-four, the ocean ready to crash in on me. Doug crossed the street first and got to the car; he thought I was right behind him.

Instead, I was going headfirst into a fast decline, where the clouds, trees, grass, and cars turn into smears, like a whipping blur. Faster than the Zipper and more nauseating.

I could feel my panic pushing me and forcing its way through my skin. Fear was taking over; devilish teeth sank into my flesh. My mouth was completely dry. I was spinning faster and faster, totally off-balance.

I had known this day would come. Jeff, the hairstylist (I think that was his name), would murder me with a knife for sure. He would cut me into tiny little pieces, fry me in a pan, and feed me to his cat. And do other unspeakable things.

The obsessive thinking escalated: *If only I had not done it; if only I could have kept my defamatory and slanderous thoughts to myself. Oh my God, why did I have to tell him that I know he's a psychopath, and that I know about the murders he has committed? Why did I have to write it all down on a yellow sticky note and throw it in the corner of his shop for him to find? I am so stupid!*

The pain and mental anguish unleashed were unbearable. I could hardly breathe. I didn't feel any air getting into my lungs. I was trying to look normal. *Where am I?* I felt paralyzed. My head was pounding. I could no longer tell the difference between an actual situation and a thought. (In OCD Land, this is referred to as Thought Action Fusion.) *Holy shit! Not even my boyfriend will know where I am when I am being chopped up into little pieces with Jeff's knife.* My mind raced and crashed into a wall. I was taken over by a dark piece of the universe that was eating me alive. I was no longer whole. I believed that my thoughts were coming from a true place. My fear built on itself with rapid fire. I was just broken pieces crashing down. I couldn't walk, talk, or move forward. I was trembling.

I was shaking uncontrollably. I started wailing, yelling, and screaming. All I could do was wail, yell, and gasp for just one rough gulp of air. I was so sad that my life was over. Doug saw me screaming and screaming in the middle of the very busy street. He saw me collapse like a clump of wet sand, no form or shape.

There was no compulsion or ritual or performance I could do to quell my anxiety, not even going back for the piece of paper. I had crossed over.

Doug wasn't sure what was going on with me, but he knew it wasn't good at all. He ran out to me. He placed his arms around my body as if to scoop me up into his. He somehow got me out of the busy street and out of oncoming traffic. He hurriedly opened our car door and got me quickly into the passenger seat. I sat there crying, yelling, and shaking.

Doug said softly and sweetly, "You're okay now, you're okay now. I promise."

This monumental psychological breakdown, this public nosedive, made it very clear to both of us that I was no longer able to function and that everything was not okay. Whatever was happening to me—to us, in all fairness—had reached proportions that we were unable to manage and that I was unable to hide. It was bigger than we were.

I could no longer keep up my well-crafted "normal front." I was sick, very sick. We were both completely exhausted and out of ideas and solutions.

· 5 ·

GETTING TO KNOW YOU

Angel on NPR

J ust days later, we were visited by an angel. Or, should I say, Doug was.

Doug was painting in his art studio in Benicia; he was developing a product line for a gift company for whom he did freelance work. We were renting a cute second-floor condo and had turned our second bedroom into his studio. Although it was a small space, it was functional, and the view was amazing. Doug worked in front of a big window that gave him a terrific view of the Benicia straits. Every day giant tankers and ships would sail by, making a beautiful and grand sight out on the water.

Doug often listened to NPR while he was working. On this particular day, a public service announcement caught his attention. The sixty-second spot went something like this: "Do you or someone you know obsess about things and can't seem to let them go? Does compulsive behavior interfere with your life? Then you may be suffering from obsessive-compulsive disorder."

Wow, he thought. *Maybe this is it. Obsessive-compulsive disorder.*

The voice on the radio continued, "If so, there is a help line that you can call to get the information you or someone you care about needs. You can find specialists in your area that can help with obsessive-compulsive disorder."

He reached for a pen and quickly jotted down the number.

As it happened, I only worked a half day that day, and when I got home I visited him like usual in his studio. He was unusually excited to see me: "I am so glad you're home; I have something to share with you." I could tell it was something big and serious. He had that *this is important* tone in his voice. He told me what he'd heard on the radio and handed me the piece of paper with the 800 number on it.

My hand trembled a little as I took the paper. I felt both excited and a little scared that there might be help out there. I could feel a little lurch of hope in my belly. Tears welled up in my eyes. I stared down at the phone and pushed each number slowly and with precision. Of course, I didn't want to make a mistake while dialing the number. Mistakes, large or small, were still fuel for my OCD; I couldn't handle being clubbed again by Sergeant.

Good fortune was upon us: the person who answered the help line told me there was an OCD specialist in my area. His name was Dr. Kalb. I immediately called his office.

Even greater—and incredible—good luck. Dr. Kalb answered his phone! Nothing about his calming and mellow voice scared me, which was unusual, because at this time everything seemed to scare me terribly. I described a little of what I'd been going through. He listened carefully and told me he could make an opening in his schedule that afternoon. I would meet with him at 2 p.m. in his Novato office. I didn't know exactly where Novato was, but he said it was about forty-five minutes away from Benicia. I did know one thing for sure: hell or high water would not keep me from getting there.

After I said thank you with all my heart and soul to Dr. Kalb, I hung up the phone, stunned in disbelief. Still in tears, I said to Doug, "He's going to meet with me today!" and fell into his arms. He gave me a strong, meaningful bear hug and offered to drive me up there. "No," I said. "I think I can drive myself, if I can just stop crying." I smiled a little at Doug and grabbed a tissue to wipe the tears off my face.

I've Been Fucking Robbed
(and the Big Reveal)

I have little memory of driving to Novato. I just seemed to appear in the parking lot in front of the brownish-red brick building that Dr. Kalb described on the phone. Somehow I found the right door with Dr. Daniel Kalb's nameplate on it.

I proceeded to sit in the small waiting room by myself. The room was welcoming. It had some small, healthy plants on a shelf, and it was painted in unobtrusive, calming tan and beige colors. But I was still nervous as hell. I sat straight up like a board, feeling the intensity surging up and down my body. I was exhausted. The circles under my eyes were deeper and darker than usual.

Sergeant was with me, of course. He asked, "What if this guy, Kalb, is a serial killer? Should you really be here in his trap?" As these thoughts circled around inside my head, I stared intently at Dr. Kalb's office door, trancelike, as though I were boring a hole through it. Then the door opened, slowly. There stood a man with a slender build, fair skin, and auburn hair. He was dressed nicely, casual in khakis and a plaid shirt. He introduced himself as Dan Kalb. I registered that the name he gave matched the name that he had given me on the phone earlier and felt relief. We shook hands.

I didn't know what to do with myself until he suggested that I come into his office. He brought me over to a chair intended for me. He opened his hand toward it, suggesting that I sit there. The chair was light orange, and it was a fairly comfortable living room–like stuffed chair that you sink into a little. In contrast, I felt stiff, and my mouth was completely dry.

We talked a little bit, the usual kind of chat to fill the new space between two people. "Did you find the place okay? Were the directions helpful?" I had gotten pretty good at chitchat, while a larger part of me was completely disconnected. I wondered if he noticed that I did not make significant eye contact.

The room was bright and sunny; it felt like healthiness took place there, the antithesis of sickly and dead, the opposite of Sick Pond. The blinds behind Dr. Kalb were wide open, and the windows were very clean; I could clearly see the Bay Area mountains. It took every bit of my resolve to stay in my seat and not run out of the room. Thoughts raced in quickly like a line of marching soldiers. *Oh my God, how am I going to do this? What if he is a serial killer?* Sergeant quickly drew up a picture of Dr. Kalb with a knife stabbing an unknown person without a face, over and over, blood splashing everywhere. *I should go. Why reveal all of my personal facts and information to a serial killer, just to make it easier for him to kill me?"* Sergeant proclaimed, "Revealing your secrets, that's what a stupid idiot would do!" I tried not to see the sharp blade, the sharp silver knife Dr. Kalb was holding up, his violent stabbing motions, and the splashing blood.

Dr. Kalb inquired a little more, but gently. I told him that I had finished college and gotten my bachelor's degree, that I had a successful career, and that I was living in Benicia with my boyfriend of many years, Doug.

Dr. Kalb, with his round brown eyes, looked right into my green eyes, the same eyes that an old boyfriend had once called green swamp water when he was mad at me. I'm sure Dr. Kalb could see that I was terrified right beyond the swamp. I had been hiding myself away in a giant safe in my head. The safe where I shoved and locked away so many secrets and so much pain. The secret world of Sergeant, the perfect predator, and the complete me that I had never revealed to anyone. All the abuse, all the rules, all my imperfections, all my fear, all of the dark corners. But Dr. Kalb had found his way in, and I could no longer keep up my front. I was now like the squishy part of a jelly bean, the inside part, with the thick candy shell gone.

Dr. Kalb asked me to fill out a questionnaire. It was one long page, and I could quickly see that the intent of the questions was to find out how deep in the woods I was. Was I call-the-paddy-wagon-to-come-pick-her-up-now-bat-shit crazy? One-Flew-Over-the-Cuckoo's-Nest crazy? I had nowhere to hide. I felt exposed, raw, cornered, and vulnerable.

Mustering up some courage (from exactly where, I had no idea), I took the test. It was called the Y-BOCS (Yale–Brown Obsessive Compulsive Scale).

To my surprise and horror, I answered yes to all of the questions. I knew this could not be good. Then I took a couple of invisible blows of truth straight to the face! I could not dodge it. The girl who strove for perfection was a derailed, tangled, fearful, knotted-up, bunchy, and unglued mess—and, yes, **CRAZY!** Gulp. *Feeling so unbearably WRONG and trembling*, I handed the test back to Dr. Kalb.

Then the tears began to pour, and I mean pour! I fell completely apart; I let go of everything—everything. I released tears held back from childhood, old tears that had been tucked away for more than thirty years, and then brand-new tears. I cried so much that I choked a little. I cried so much that my nose began to run. This release of CRAZY was overwhelming. My whole face was wet.

Dr. Kalb handed me a box of tissues and sat calmly, not creepily like a serial killer would, I thought to myself. What was amazing was that I did not feel judgment from him. It felt as though if I had had to cry into the night, he would have sat there with me. Although I felt exposed and vulnerable, I did not feel threatened.

Next, he said calmly and directly, "You are suffering from OCD, obsessive-compulsive disorder." He went on to say that OCD was a real medical condition. He told me that having OCD was not my fault.

As soon as he said those words, "**NOT MY FAULT,**" I cried harder and louder than I ever had. I just sat there and wailed; I could not talk at all. I could only reply by sucking in more air as I tried to look at him.

He went on to say, "Obsessive-compulsive disorder is an anxiety disorder characterized by recurrent thoughts, feelings, ideas, or sensations or behaviors that a person feels driven to perform. Compulsions are a strong, usually irresistible, impulse to perform an act, especially one that is irrational or contrary to one's will."

The relief was overwhelming. I looked up at Dr. Kalb.

"Do you mean it was OCD that made me so sick and hopeless for so many years? Dr. Kalb, I have OCD really, really bad. What am I going to do? I feel like no thoughts are my own!" I yelled through my tears, "and I am fucking tired of it!"

I think that even the mountains on the other side of the thick glass window heard those words come roaring out of me. His empathetic and nonjudgmental eyes confirmed that I was in trouble and reassured me that I had come to the right place.

Next, he said, "How does it feel to have accomplished so much and have had such success in your life, while only having used 10 percent of your brain, with the other 90 percent used for OCD?"

I thought to myself, *It's a fucking miracle.*

I had never seen myself as accomplished; I had always felt broken, deeply flawed, and most of the time disorganized, unsteady, barely holding on, and mostly not lovable. But looking at my life with this new information from Dr. Kalb made me think of four things:

- "Oh my God, this doctor is right; I was only functioning with 10 percent of my brain power!"

- Next, a glimmer of hope. I thought, "If the other 90 percent were available, I would be able to do so much more with my life. Could I even enjoy my life?"

- Then I felt utter sadness. For the first time, I clearly saw that OCD, this new title for my private hell, had been consuming me.

- Finally, I felt the deepest rage that I had ever felt, a volcano erupting out of every cell in my body. "Dr. Kalb," I yelled through my tears, "I've been fucking robbed!"

All at once, I could feel my inner warrior surface. I was open to it, and it was the coolest feeling in the world. I wasn't alone anymore. Everyone has a first day on the job, and this was mine. It was as if one clock stopped and another one started. I would fight, climb, and kick my way out of this prison called OCD and do whatever was necessary to get the 90 percent back that was rightfully mine.

Dr. Kalb then asked me, "What does your OCD look like?"

I thought, *He's like a Monkey; a vicious Monkey that's always up to no good, a clever Monkey that's always running around my brain and can't be caught.*

I've Been Fucking Robbed

· · · · · · · ·

KEY POINTS TO REMEMBER

· · · · · · · ·

"It's not your fault." When I heard those words from Dr. Kalb, I felt relief. **Obsessive-compulsive disorder** (OCD) *is not your fault either.* It is a chemical imbalance in your brain. It is a medical condition.

OCD is characterized by unreasonable thoughts and fears of imagined catastrophes (obsessions) that lead you to do repetitive, bizarre, or self-destructive behaviors (compulsions).

It takes courage to say, "I have a problem and I need help." This is a sign of strength, not weakness. Denial is a strong force that can get in the way of your becoming healthy and evolving into a more joyous existence.

Change often happens when not changing becomes more painful than changing.

My "abuser" had power when I kept my relationship with him (in my case, he's male) a secret. My abuser, my OCD, had power when I saw no other way to go, when I saw no other options.

It is sometimes frightening to get raw and exposed with yourself or even someone you trust, but often a truthful place is the best place to start real change.

Giving a name to your tormentor may help you to separate from it/him/her. My OCD is called Monkey. That's the name I thought described him best. This separation, of giving him a name, brought some awareness and relief to the forefront.

OCD finds its way in and usually begins with one grain of truth. A lot of lies begin this way. The grain of truth is the hook to get you to buy in to the empty promise and begin your performance. For instance, "it's good to be clean." Sure, this is an agreeable point; however, you need to look out because OCD is an exaggerator. He grabs your hand and runs wildly away with you to a place where you're further away from reality and smack in the heart of obsessive-compulsive behavior.

The test that I took to evaluate my current state with my OCD/Monkey was called the Y-BOCS test. It stands for the Yale–Brown Obsessive Compulsive Scale. You can google it and find the test online if you wish to take it.

To start heading in a healthy direction, I had to have a moment of clarity and summon my inner warrior. (More about this later . . .)

The other important thing I learned is that with us OCDers our brain's alarm system is broken. My internal alarm blares, sounds off, and warns me of past, present, or future imminent danger. The fear I feel is real. (I have even seen studies in which you can see the actual brain of the OCDers' mental circuit board lighting up; it looks like a lightning storm—our brain is unfortunately misfiring.) The alarm's broken. It's like a smoke alarm going off in someone's house, yet in reality there is no smoke or fire. It's just that darn broken alarm again! Just where do I go from here?

Is There a Cure?

My second appointment with Dr. Kalb was at his Benicia office. I couldn't believe my luck that he had this second office just a mile from where Doug and I lived. His office was down by the water, and it was much like the other one, with healthy plants and good lighting. The room was decorated in neutral tones, which made me feel calm (unlike being with Monkey, who made me always feel alarmed, like the color red continuously flashing). Dr. Kalb was again in a comfortable but professional outfit: brown pants, a plaid shirt, and a sweater—sort of like a middle-aged trustworthy uncle.

The weird thing about Monkey, what Sergeant morphed into, was that because he had been the power player, the authority figure I had listened to for all these years, "telling" on him to Dr. Kalb seemed very wrong and strange, almost taboo. I felt guilty exposing him. But I knew that to get better I had to get beyond that.

We Americans want the Cure. We pay big bucks for the cure. Advertisers sell you the cure. It is how the popular culture American society is set up.

The search for a fix, for a ready solution to what ails, has become a uniquely American undertaking, an ingrained part of consumer culture, as prevalent as the nearest diet workshop or plastic surgeon.

**—CAROLINE KNAPP,
*DRINKING: A LOVE STORY***

In the beginning, Dr. Kalb and I met once a week. He was a careful listener and had sensitive radar for Monkey; he could spot him, see him coming, and I knew he could teach me this skill.

Dr. Kalb explained that OCD comes in all different forms; it all depends on the person. Some people have a fear of contaminants and infection, trying to sterilize their surroundings to prevent contamination. Some people even move from state to state to run away from imaginary but powerfully real-seeming germs. Or they are cursed with the need to wash their hands over and over again, continuing even when their hands become dry, cracked, and bloody.

Other people are afraid that while they were driving, they hit somebody on the road, so they drive the same route over and over trying to find their victim. I realized that while we OCDers don't fear the same things, we all want the same peace, the same certainty that everything is going to be okay. That's why we do such crazy things. We participate in our obsessions and compulsions so that the torment and fear will stop. I felt very connected with other OCDers. My heart was sad for them. It blew my mind that millions of people suffer from OCD. That seemed awfully unfair and unjust.

When Dr. Kalb told me about other types of OCD that people have (while always being careful and preserving privacy with his patients), their OCD sounded a little silly to me, not nearly as real as mine. I wished that I could tell them the truth, that there was nothing for them to be afraid of. But I also knew that for someone who is afraid of cotton balls, they can have sharp, little, puncturing teeth that the rest of us don't see. I felt like my OCD was different. It was real. I had everything to be afraid of.

One day, many sessions into my therapy, I rather naively asked Dr. Kalb, "Is there a cure? Moles can be removed from your face; can OCD be removed?" He replied, "On very rare occasions, it can go away completely. Often adding medication to therapy can be helpful. You can make even chronic OCD a whole lot better and much more manageable."

It was clear that getting better was going to be a lot of hard work, especially starting from where I was. It would be the fight of a lifetime.

I was ready to take it, it was the only choice I saw, yet I was terrified at the same time.

Spying and Exposure

The obstacle is the path.

—ZEN PROVERB

I once heard a story about a family in my neighborhood who brought inside two cocoons that were just about to hatch. They watched as the first one began to open, and the butterfly inside squeezed very slowly and painfully through a tiny hole that it had chewed in one end of the encapsulating cocoon. After lying exhausted for about ten minutes following its agonizing emergence, the butterfly finally flew out the open window on its beautiful wings.

The family decided to help the second butterfly so that it would not have to go through such an excruciating ordeal. As the butterfly began to emerge, they carefully sliced open the cocoon with a razor blade, doing the equivalent of a cesarean section. The second butterfly never did sprout wings, and in about ten minutes, instead of flying away, it quietly died.

The family asked a biologist friend to explain what had happened.

The scientist said that the difficult struggle to emerge from the small hole actually pushes liquids from deep inside the butterfly's body cavity into the tiny capillaries in the wings, where they harden to complete the healthy and beautiful adult butterfly.

WITHOUT THE STRUGGLE, THERE ARE NO WINGS! I saw myself as the patient and the surgeon!

Dr. Kalb said that we were going to start with homework. *Jesus!* I thought. *My life is already so jam-packed and now I have to add homework to it! Fuck!* He told me what we were going to do and why it would be helpful. That was key for me—understanding the underlying purpose. I never saw the purpose of algebra, which made it difficult for me to click into. He explained that we'd both have to agree to each homework assignment given.

The first assignment he gave me would be to take notes on myself between now and the next session. I said, "Sort of like spying on myself?" He continued, "In this exercise you will observe yourself, taking notes on your activities and responses. You will become more conscious of yourself, more aware." I was to record any thoughts that brought me anxiety. I would give them a number from one to ten, with one being low anxiety and ten being out of my mother-flipping mind. I would also record how I handled my anxiety and how much time I spent trying to please Monkey (my OCD) to make things better or at least tolerable.

I agreed to give this homework a try although it sounded very cumbersome and certainly not my first choice of things to do. But I was committed to the plan and I realized that the route I was on presently was no longer working. I was open to his idea.

So off I went, out into the world taking notes on my anxious thoughts and activities. I carried a little spiral notebook with me, and I was taking notes on myself all the time! Recording. Recording. Recording.

For instance, I jotted down an anxiety rating of six over the voice-mails that I had to leave for a coworker. Sometimes I would replay and rerecord my messages twenty times so that they would be absolutely clear and perfect for Monkey's approval. Finally, after much time and effort, Monkey raised the flag that said I had left the perfect message and I could be released. Once I achieved his approval, I would move on to the next thing. If I didn't allow myself to check the voicemail messages (which is the nonaction Dr. Kalb wanted eventually), this would have caused me level ten anxiety, and at this time that was unthinkable. Just taking all the notes seemed more than enough.

Because Monkey was so jacked up by this time in my life, even tying my shoes had to be to his standards. Everything had to be to Monkey's standards. If I didn't obey, no matter how big or small on the outside, I would have level ten anxieties (the painful and debilitating mental zaps like in the game Operation). So I did everything the way Monkey wanted it, every second of every day.

By the end of the first week, my notebook was filled with page after page of situations of my unforgivable imperfections and trying to keep Monkey from complete rage on my ass. Pretty much second to second, I was making mistakes in Monkey's eyes, and I had to keep redoing just about everything, even how I swallowed, how my teeth touched (which, due to anxiety, I had significantly ground down while sleeping at night), how my hair was hanging, what was in my purse and how it was organized, how I was sitting, what I was saying, what I was writing, how I was talking—it all had to be approved by my overlord, OCD, aka Sergeant, aka MONKEY!

I began to see that I was in a continuous loop with my OCD and that it was taking all my time. One obsession would get quelled, and another one would arrive on my mental doorstep. It was a procession of my flaws, one after the next, on an ongoing conveyor belt.

I just wanted to do what Monkey wanted me to do so I wouldn't have to deal with his unloading of unbearable grief and taunts of things inevitably to come due to a poor and unforgivable performance. Everything from drowning kittens to killing my mom to having a serial killer slice me at the throat. Monkey was hyperintelligent and strategic; he carefully siphoned my imagination and used it against me. I thought to myself, *How much further along I would be if I could get some of my imagination back and for better and more joyful things.* I also wanted to be more available to my relationship with Doug and more available to life. Get out of my acrylic box and take down some of the buffering walls.

At my next session, I showed Dr. Kalb the pages with all of my oddities, and I got to see how much time I wasted on all of this. I was shocked at all the things I did every day just to be compliant. I was embarrassed as well, sharing all of this with him. He helped me to see my data, pen on paper, as an outsider would. It was as though we each had on our white lab coats while reviewing the interesting findings.

He explained that this was the key to healing: If I could get just one millimeter of distance from my OCD, that gap could grow, and that is where I would start making healthy changes. But it seemed so far away. I had been under the command of my Sergeant and then into Monkey for more than twenty-some years!

Dr. Kalb explained that what we were looking at on these pages were obsessions and compulsions, the root of my OCD. The obsessions being what my mind fixated on that made me anxious, and in an effort to neutralize the obsessions, I did my compulsions (my perfect performances).

"Do you think Monkey makes good decisions for you? Look at your pages; is this what you want to be doing? Do you want to try something else? You have been doing what Monkey wants you to for a long time."

"Too long! Too goddamn long, Dr. Kalb!"

"What would have happened if you hadn't participated in this long list of time-consuming and time-wasting activities?" Dr. Kalb asked. "Do you think you would have survived it?"

I didn't even pause. "No! I wouldn't have been able to take it." If I hadn't done what Monkey asked and the way he wanted it, he would have tortured me. Just moving on without Monkey's approval was unthought of and excruciating. I tried it in little ways in the past, to test the waters, to see what would happen if I didn't please Monkey. There were times that I dropped to the floor in mental anguish and found myself in the fetal position screaming and crying.

Monkey would tower over me and yell and scream and keep reminding me of the unforgivable mistakes that I had made and the doom that would come because of my careless incompetence. Monkey held the stick—I just cowered. This was our relationship. I really didn't know how to stop allowing it.

Dr. Kalb pointed out that the compulsions by themselves, performed strictly for their own sake, did not get me out of Monkey's trap. Indeed, such performance was part of the trap! Whoa. *I was seeing the big picture.*

I met with Dr. Kalb once a week at first. And I kept at my homework, spying on myself and taking lots of notes. **Over several weeks, the homework evolved, but I stuck to it**.

We created an *exposure hierarchy list* detailing the main situations or sources of anxiety that trigger my fear (OCD), arranged in order from lowest amount of anxiety to the highest. (I believe it was a scale of 1 to 100.)

We started simply from the lowest number. It seemed more humane working from the bottom up. Slowly and steadily, I started to incorporate not allowing myself to do my compulsions for relief; this was the **exposure** (so *not* fun). For instance, leave a message for a coworker and not allow myself to check it. Just send the baby on through.

The more I could expose myself to the unwanted experiences and the unwanted feelings that arose from not doing my compulsions, the more *desensitized* I would become to the stimulus. I pushed myself hard to work my way up the list of each trigger, and over time, each trigger I worked with would bring less anxiety. Interestingly, as time went on, because of exposure therapy, my stress level numbers went down with the same stimulus.

Somehow, without looking, Dr. Kalb always knew exactly when our hour was close to being up, and he'd always leave enough time to explain my next homework assignment in detail.

By now, I had gotten pretty high up my exposure hierarchy list. My next BIG homework assignment had to do with the little notes that terrified me the most. Just thinking of little scraps of paper could make me cry. For instance, collecting and organizing receipts was an incredibly difficult and mostly avoided task. It would send my skin crawling. At this time in my life, I was always feeling like I wrote something defamatory on pieces of paper and that I left the notes everywhere for serial killers to find and come torture and kill me. Again, my negligence leads to my very end.

Dr. Kalb's and my exposure homework assignment would take place at our local Raley's grocery store. Before going into the store, I would purposely write something on a yellow sticky note and bring it with me. I would then choose a place to leave the yellow sticky note behind. I would have to risk the wrong person finding it. No matter what, I could not go back into the store to retrieve the note.

The first time Dr. Kalb described this, I thought, *This guy is nuts!* But what I said was, "Holy shit, Dr. Kalb, this homework is going to be so hard. It sounds worse than giving birth to a baby rhinoceros, horn first." He told me that I might see other people's sticky notes around the store because he gives lots of OCDers around town similar homework. I didn't know if he was joking or serious. Either way I thought he was both cruel and outrageous! He said that the purpose of this exposure homework was to desensitize me. But it sounded as though exposure homework was created to torture me!

I wasn't sure that I was up for this. Dr. Kalb told me that just like anything else, the more I practiced exposure therapy, the better I'd become at it. No matter what, I could not react to Monkey by going to retrieve the note. I had to risk the consequences of what would happen by leaving the note there. At that moment, to my mind, Dr. Kalb was asking me to accept the fact that I could get murdered!

This was a big deal. It was going to be the first time that I intentionally gave Monkey the middle finger. I felt terrified.

Dr. Kalb said, "Leave the note and say to Monkey, agree with him really and say, 'Yes, Monkey, a mad, crazy serial killer is going to find my note, read it, find me, and kill me.' This will make you very uncomfortable. It goes against all your instincts, but you must do it."

I knew I was going into the fight of a lifetime, which would bring on a full-frontal attack by Monkey! I desperately wanted to be tough enough to pull it off. I knew I would have to access my inner warrior, and that started with belief in myself (what I had so little of). After all, OCD is a doubting disease in that you doubt yourself and doubt what you have done or what you didn't do. Just so much doubt and uncertainty. Rather than fueling doubt, I had to fuel belief in myself, and this wasn't going to be easy. I had been submissive for just so long. *I remember Dr. Kalb's last words at that appointment: "Do not service your OCD."* Gulp.

Spying and Exposure

· · · · · · · ·

KEY POINTS TO REMEMBER

· · · · · · · ·

Dr. Kalb's encouragement and OCD expertise helped me greatly on my path to wellness, my first steps out of the OCD circus. I knew it was going to be a struggle; however, I had faith that I was on the path to my freedom and that it would be worth the effort.

He assigned me homework that he called *exposure therapy*. It was not a pleasant experience, and I dreaded it! It involved two new things: spying and exposure. Just letting things be—oh my gosh, this went against Monkey big time!

What is involved in exposure therapy, anyway?

- **Spying**—This is where I built my impartial spectator rather than just getting swept up into an OCD trance (again!). How much time do I spend on my obsessions? How much time do I spend on my compulsions? I learned to watch and observe myself just enough to create a little distance.

- **Exposure**—I made an exposure hierarchy list and started at the bottom of the list, exposing myself to what caused the least amount of anxiety. Not doing my compulsions made me uncomfortable (let me rephrase that, made me climb the walls); Monkey sounded all the alarms in my being. However, doing my compulsions (what I do to feel better and lessen the anxiety) performed strictly for their own sake would not get me out of the OCD trap. Indeed, such performance was part of the trap.

- **Investigative Research**—By spying on myself and exposing myself to my OCD hotspots (my anxiety trigger areas) from least difficult to most difficult, I could begin the learning process, taking stock of myself and seeing my own behavior, rather than just caving and participating in the loop.

    - Where are my OCD hotspots?

    - What is the level of anxiety that they bring if I don't allow myself to do my compulsions?

- **My OCD Cycle**—Obsessions are what cause anxiety and take over my mind and compulsions are my attempt to temporarily quell the obsessions and the anxiety they bring.

This fact-gathering process was amazing; the data about my OCD was interesting. In the past, I had just always done what Monkey wanted me to do and away I went! Now I was prepared and taking notes on my own behavior. I was sitting in a different seat and beginning the process of change and quite possibly shifting my behavior.

I once heard this joke: "How do you eat an elephant?" The answer: "One bite at a time." But in my case, the elephant was a MONKEY! He tasted nasty, too!

Giving Monkey the Middle Finger

At first, exposure is awful and the last thing you want to do; it seems counterintuitive. Why take on more stress for yourself? However, as you will see, in the end exposure is your friend and your way out of the OCD circus.

❖ ❖ ❖ ❖ ❖ ❖ ❖

Back to the story and way up in my exposure hierarchy: there I was in my car in front of Raley's writing my first intentional yellow sticky note for my assigned (and agreed-to!) exposure homework.

I wrote down just my first name, Kirsten, but I *felt* as though I was also writing down my full address and bank account and the words "Come kill me, motherfucker!" I checked and rechecked to make sure it was only my first name. My palms were sweaty. My heart practically exploded with the thought of purposely dropping off the note somewhere inside.

I went into the store, got a cart, and headed to the produce section. My eyes darted around, and I probably looked pretty suspicious. I know I felt suspicious. I walked over to the tomatoes and carrots looking as natural as I could. I picked up one or two tomatoes as if to examine them. I also looked at the per-pound price at the top of the mountain of bananas. I made sure that the bunch I grabbed had no bruising. Even during this homework assignment, I was compelled to find perfect-looking fruit. Then, I found my spot; it was going to be in the broccoli. The broccoli heads looked like miniature trees, and I felt like I was in a plane flying above them. The mist that shot out was like jungle mist. I was in the plane, and I had to drop a bomb from above! I had to drop the yellow sticky note right on top of the broccoli. I *almost did it* five times but backed out each time. Unsuccessful, I left the broccoli, my heart beating hard and fast. I spent some downtime with the melons, pineapples, and tangerines. I put some tangerines in a plastic bag, after fighting to open the slippery bag. I thought I was a convincing actress. This would distract anyone who might be watching me.

Finally, I found my way back to the broccoli; I was trying to find courage as my heart pounded through my T-shirt. I took the folded, incriminating note out of my front pocket, got my hand misted, and then, *pow!* I dropped the note right on top of the broccoli. I wanted to pick the note back up, but I heard Dr. Kalb's voice saying, "Have the dreaded experience. Risk it." I took off like a shot and left my cart standing there in the aisle, alone.

I walked out of the produce section with dread and headed to the boxes of cereal in a nearby aisle. I wanted to be near something familiar. I started to cry. My head was spinning; I felt absolutely sick! It was driving me crazy that I couldn't go back to my note and retrieve it. But I knew I had to do it. I had to. The desire to be well was what I leaned into.

As you know, Monkey made mental movies for me. First, it was someone stabbing me. "You are such a fool to have left your bank account number on your note and you wrote, 'Come kill me, motherfucker.' You are asking for your own death, you stupid whore." I was in a mental battle with Monkey. Intrusive thoughts flashed in front of my eyes as I tried to read the words *Frosted Flakes* and look at Tony the Tiger through my tears. Nobody could see my invisible opponent. I felt like I was falling forward and then falling backward. I tried to stay in the moment and solidify my vision and not get taken away by the images Monkey provided.

I started chanting quietly to myself, "It's okay, it's okay, it's okay. It's just Monkey; he's making this up." Monkey was squeezing the life and vibrancy out of me in a calculating and callous way. "Go get the note and you won't be killed, fool. Go get the **MOTHERFUCKING NOTE, YOU GODDAMN BITCH!**"

I ran straight out of Raley's and to my car. Once inside, I started crying again. I kept envisioning the note I had left there in the mist. I could see someone's big, burly hands picking up the note and reading it. I could see my bank account drawn down to zero, and it was all my fault.

I sobbed for a long time. I shook and cried and tried to get Monkey out of my head the best I could.

Monkey's specialty was barraging me with frightening images. Monkey was skilled and made compelling and horrific, propaganda-filled movies. I had to sit back and watch them. I remember Dr. Kalb saying, "The idea is to see the distraction as it is, a distraction." He was a tricky little bastard. How the hell was I supposed to get out of this sticky OCD web custom designed for me?

Amazingly, after I don't know how long, I eventually drove away without going back for the note. My head was pounding and my fear was overwhelming, but I pushed through. I did obsess about the note frequently and for many days and felt very stressed about my impending doom and the serial killer who was coming my way. I obsessed about the note on the broccoli when I was on the toilet, in the shower, in bed, in work meetings. I obsessed while driving, making dinner, and doing the dishes.

So maybe you, my fellow OCDer, are doubtful of yourself, and you say, "Kirsten, this is all very interesting, and maybe *managed exposure therapy* may work for you, but I've thought about it and I just don't think I can do exposure therapy. It's just too hard and scary. It just seems easier to do my compulsions. Why make my OCD mad and myself more miserable?" I say, "Because managed exposure therapy practice will build up your inner warrior and build your resilience." Then perhaps you say, "Growing a warrior within myself that can handle exposure therapy just isn't in the cards for me." Then I share this amazing story with you about growth coming in against all perceived odds.

Archaeologists found *tree seeds* that were stowed for two thousand years in a clay jar. No one believed that after lying dormant these seeds could sprout, much less grow. A botanical researcher named Elaine planted one of the seeds to see what would happen. That seed grew into a large tree that continues to thrive to this day. It is the oldest known tree seed to germinate. Miracle? Desire to live and be alive? You tell me.

Growth and evolution can happen if you believe and you allow it to. Your inner warrior is your superhero within you. It's your fighter, the one that avenges what you have lost and the one that marches on with the strong shoulders. You, my friend, are worth fighting for. It's one step at a time, heading in the right direction toward your freedom.

Monkey Is at the Door.
Are You Going to Answer It?

You can live with the pain, you can live with it. It is unpleasant, but going the way Monkey wants you to go IS NOT AN OPTION if you wish to be released.

❖   ❖   ❖   ❖   ❖   ❖   ❖

I was so relieved when I finally got to see Dr. Kalb again. I told him what I had done.

"You stood up to Monkey! Does it feel good? This was a big challenge for you. You proved that you can do it!"

I cried and smiled a shaky smile, as I felt an overwhelming rush of relief and then a dose of sadness because I was letting go of the familiar of a twenty-something-year habit. I was trying to leave a terribly mean friend that I'd had a relationship with for years. It's a bittersweet feeling with a strange sadness. It's unpleasant, and it feels weird to stand up where I used to cower. It was a weird sensation building my inner warrior, and it was equally as weird feeling the little seeds of courage growing again inside me.

I told Dr. Kalb what I was feeling.

He said, "The best way to get rid of the pain of your obsessions is to not do your compulsions, no matter how difficult they are to resist. I know it seems counterintuitive and not what you would prefer to do. It is unpleasant, but the option of going the way Monkey wants you to go is not healthy. Mentally, piece by piece, effort by effort, homework assignment by homework assignment, you will be creating new patterns in which you process the OCD data, the telecasts you get from Monkey."

Like changing the hard drive of a computer, I knew this was going to take a long time, but strangely I was still up for the challenge. For months, I was reminded of the note I left behind in Raley's and all the terrible things that were going to happen to me and my family because of the note getting into the wrong person's hands. *I should not have left it there. I may never have peace. I may never be able to stop thinking about this note.* Yes, I did the homework, but it felt foreign and dreadful. The reward from this monumental exposure therapy was not immediate or pleasant. I just had to have faith that I was going in the healthy direction.

Next up: Habituation.

Here's an example of how it works (I've adapted this from the book *Brain Lock*). Say you moved into an apartment right next to the train tracks. At first, the noise of the trains going by would be noticeable, bothersome, and make it hard to sleep. Instead of reaching for earplugs or moving out of the apartment, you just let the trains and their distracting noise go by. After you are exposed to this ongoing, bothersome stimulus, the sound of the train coming and going seems to fade away. If not completely at first, at least it will move into the background and become less likely to grab your attention as time goes on. This is called *habituation*.

For me, Monkey owned the train, he was the conductor, and he decided when the train would come and go and how loud it would be. Exposure therapy required that I let the train go by without doing something to make the train or the noise stop. I learned to live with the noise, rather than trying to stuff my ears with cotton. This way of behaving was counterintuitive because I wanted to stuff my ears immediately to stop the annoying sound and all my uncomfortableness. But if I did that, the sound would get louder and louder, and I would need more and more cotton. *I realized that the more I played with Monkey, the more I stayed with Monkey.* It was like those colorful woven Chinese finger puzzles that you could win as a prize at the carnival: Your natural inclination is to pull your fingers out right away. But doing this only tightens the trap. Instead, you have to relax into it to free your fingers.

Deep down, past my anxiety, I knew that if I could better understand the cause (Monkey), then I could try to fix my problem. I had to be like an engineer studying the inner workings of a clock. I needed to study my opponent. I needed to learn to speak "Monkey."

With Monkey jumping wildly around constantly, being a slippery asshole, and wanting to remain in power, how could I get a good look? He was a crafty S.O.B. that knew how to dodge, and he was a mercurial entity at that. I needed more knowledge about my opponent than one-hour therapy sessions and my homework could accomplish. I was thirsting for more knowledge.

I went to the self-help section of Barnes & Noble and searched for a book that would do a jumping jack in front of my face and say, "Here I am, Kirsten. I am the one that you need, pick me." I was hoping that my angels would be here again, like they were when Doug heard the OCD public service announcement on NPR that turned us on to these words strung together: *obsessive-compulsive disorder.*

Scanning, scanning, fingering over the books, and *boom!* It grabbed me: Dr. Jeffrey Schwartz's *Brain Lock.* Yep, the title spoke to me. My brain was locked!

I thumbed through some pages, and this book looked useful. I took it home and showed Doug my new find. I said, "I'm not sure why, but I think this book is going to help me in a profound way." I held it to my chest like an evangelist holds a Bible. It felt like the next right step on my journey to health.

Brain Lock offered concrete steps to follow when Monkey was knocking at the door and trying craftily to capture my attention. I couldn't believe what I read from one page to the next. All these issues that I felt I was suffering alone were also popular with other OCDers. There was even a list that cited common compulsions. My mind was opened a bit to see that others, not just me, were doing some of the same stupid shit and participating in strange behaviors. Seeing this didn't make my obsessions and compulsions go away, but they brought me some deep awareness about my particular condition and the other obsessions and compulsions that other OCDers are dealing with, too.

When reading *Brain Lock*, I could clearly attach my own behaviors to what I was reading and see myself in them vividly. I was really getting into some interesting material, and my white lab coat was on big time!

There was everything from checking compulsions to asking over and over for reassurance to touching, counting, and tapping! This author/doctor was really onto something. It was clear to me that I was an "El Supremo Checker!" He also described other manifestations of OCD that weren't dead ringers for me, but boy, could I relate to the suffering!

"Excessive ruminating about relationships, self-image, and self-esteem."

Hello, high school! Basically, Hello, OCD! It was more apparent now than ever that I REALLY HAD IT. Now how the fuck do I get rid of you? Riddles inside of riddles inside of riddles. Scribble, I tell ya. No straight lines! How I wanted those straight lines!

Sometimes I would get confused and say, "Is this real, or is this Monkey?" Remember, I told myself Monkey was a tricky bastard and he always began with an element of truth, and for me, anyway, he was super crafty on getting my emotional buy-in to the material. I learned that almost always if I thought it might be Monkey, it usually was.

Also, Dr. Schwartz turned me on to the concept of the four *R*s he created:

- **Relabel:** Basically, you say, "These intrusive urges and thoughts are the result of OCD."

- **Reattribute:** Remind yourself that chemicals are misfiring in your brain. That's all that it is.

- **Refocus:** Do another behavior; go in another direction than what OCD is demanding.

- **Revalue:** Remind yourself that this is OCD. Do not take it at face value. It holds no significance by itself.

Doing the four *R*s took a lot of awareness, navigation, and hard work! But if I didn't do these steps, I knew I would be swept into the trance yet again and Monkey would win. It felt incredible to finish the four *R*s, those chronological steps, and not trip backward into the Monkey trance. Each little victory gave me more faith in myself and helped my inner warrior grow. Grow, warrior seed, grow!

Monkey Is at the Door.
Are You Going to Answer It?

•••••••

KEY POINTS TO REMEMBER

•••••••

At first, it felt weird to stand up to Monkey, my abuser, and it was very unpleasant. Perhaps I even had a bit of sadness in trying to let go of the familiar. Our bizarre and twisted relationship was familiar, regardless of how unhealthy it was. Monkey was, for lack of a better word, a habit. I was the addict, and Monkey trance is the place where I was swept away for so many, many years.

Initially, I saw Monkey as my opponent. I wanted to learn everything that I could about him. Sort of like how a football team observes closely the other team's plays and strategies so that they can be victorious.

I looked for resources; I tried to educate myself so I could better understand the inner workings of my opponent. I set out on my investigative path of awareness. I was building my awareness arsenal.

Four big, important steps that I learned from the book *Brain Lock* are worth memorizing and using immediately: Relabel, Reattribute, Refocus, and Revalue. These are my *and your* four **R**s.

Monkey was an abuser. He was an abuser of time, well-being, and mental health. These were just for starters, and just as there are all kinds of offenders, Monkey was a mind offender (a soul and spirit offender). He was also a sadistic sociopath, but more about this later . . .

Creating an exposure hierarchy and facing fears at first seems impossible, but in the long game, doing it is so worth the time.

Habituation: Remember that *not doing your OCD urges* can be a wonderful neutralizer. Like baking soda to a sour stomach.

El Supremo Thinking — 1998: Thirty-Two Years Old

I began to see that I had **rigid blueprints** in my mind that the world, everyone in it, and I were supposed to follow. For instance, the engagement ring Doug and I chose had to be "el supremo."

On the way home after purchasing it in the SF diamond district, I told Doug I thought we might have made a $4,000 mistake. I carried on and on about how I didn't think that it was perfect enough. I was thinking and rethinking. I stared and stared at it and could see only its imperfection. I cried all the way home and at home. I asked Doug if he thought that this had anything to do with OCD or if the ring really was that imperfect. He was so mentally worn out by then that he was listless and didn't know what to tell me. He went to bed sad, and I went to bed feeling like the biggest, most unappreciative asshole there ever was. We kept the ring.

The next time I saw Dr. Kalb, I told him what had happened. After our chat, it was clear to me that OCD had once again come to ruin a beautiful day.

Doug and I went to Kauai a few weeks later, and I was pretty sure that that was where he and I would get engaged, but I kept my mouth shut.

I was a wreck trying to navigate through the airport, OCD giving me a machine-gun attack with questions. *Did you leave the stove on? Do you have your boarding pass? Is that TSA worker your serial killer?* An ongoing litany of fears took me out of the moment and deep into Monkey trance.

As you can imagine, flying was tough for me because I felt 100 percent out of control, and I had to sit still for hours in my own head. My repetitive thoughts were: *Our lives are in the hands of a stranger, the captain, an unknown face. What if he has been drinking? What if he has a death wish and today is his day?*

But this time I'd come prepared. I'd brought a little hand puzzle to keep me occupied and distracted during the flight. I was *refocusing* and proud of myself. All of my pent-up and wily energy went into pushing the orange square plastic pieces around feverishly as Doug tried to sleep. When I got bored with the puzzle, I kept compulsively checking the seat pocket in front of me. I wanted to make sure that I did not write down and then carelessly leave something defamatory for the serial killer to find when he sat in my seat on the next flight. I knew that I had an exposure therapy opportunity. I could write a sticky note and just leave it in the pocket. But that was WAY out of my reach; my inner superhero just wasn't there yet.

On to more interesting stuff, one evening while Doug and I were out on the beach in front on our hotel, he got down on one knee in the sand, with the starry sky and a full white moon above him. Doug nervously told me a little story about how he'd come to Hawaii the first time with his high school buddies and kept fantasizing about being in that paradise with a girlfriend instead of a bunch of guys. "This is that time," he said. "I am with the girl I love. Kirsten, will you marry me?"

I wanted to have the perfect response and be perfect for him—"el supremo." And I was terrified. I looked up at the moon to try to soak in all the magic, and all I could see was what Monkey provided: black Hefty bags floating by one by one in a line in front of the glowing moonlight. They were coming in from infinity in the jet-black sky, blocking the stars and distracting me from Doug and this moment. What was going on?

"Yes, Doug, I would love to marry you." Thank God the words came out right. I did not want to ruin this like I'd ruined the experience with buying the ring.

I thought to myself, as I winced at the moon and the Hefty bags, *This is OCD, this is my brain misfiring, this is Monkey being an asshole at a very important time for Doug and me.* I tried to keep my anxiety about the bags to myself and looked directly into Doug's eyes and gave him a sincere smile as each bag appeared and floated by behind him. I wanted to swat at them like a cat swats, and knock each one far away into oblivion. But I knew that making a swatting motion in front of Doug would give me away.

The once IMPERFECT ring he placed on my finger looked stunning; it shined beautifully in the moonlight, and for a minute I saw its beauty that was always there and forgot that it was the "bad ring." For just a moment, everything was okay—like balm had filled in all the cracks.

The next day I told Doug that I had to find a bookstore with the book *Brain Lock*. I wished that I would have packed it for the trip. With some searching, we found it at a little island bookstore. I liked to hold on to it and refer to it. It helped to remind me of what was going on and how to manage. During our vacation, I did a lot of journaling by the pool and tried to streamline my stress and thoughts onto the page.

I was awkward at letting go and enjoying the trip, but I tried. I tried so hard not to think, but just to be. Sometimes it even worked when I stopped thinking so much.

A Special Blend of Wedding Jitters

Monkey saw the savory selection before him that only a wedding can provide: stress, importance, performance, organization, perfection, control, lack of control, timing. He was there. Monkey was dressed for the all-time el supremo occasion, wearing his glittery red vest and making small circles with his cane. "Would not miss this for my life. These are the things that make for a perfect party. Fertile ground, and all you need is me."

After much consideration, Doug and I decided that our wedding ceremony would take place near Chicago. It made much more sense for the two of us to fly there than to ask a large group of people to fly out to California. Thank God that both of our mothers offered to pay for the wedding, even though it is customary for the father of the bride to pay. Our fathers chose not to contribute.

The calendar was marked for Saturday, July 26, 1998. All the wedding day preparation backed out from there. I was very familiar with this kind of planning approach because it's how I ran large projects at the toy company I was working for.

Doug and I selected the Danada House in Wheaton, Illinois, for our location. This 1940s property consisted of a big white country house on several acres of both open and manicured land. The house was decorated with antiques that had no dust on them. The home itself had many rooms and nooks and crannies to go exploring in.

In front of the house, there were horse stables and open space. In the back of the house, there was a man-made pond with floating lily pads in it and dragonflies enjoying their life. It couldn't have been a more perfect setting for Doug and me to exchange our vows, and the moms agreed.

Ah, but Monkey. During the preparations, Dr. Kalb continued to help me become more cognizant of my actions. I knew that I still needed help. For a long time, I didn't want to take or try any medication. Taking medication would have meant "admitting" that I was a mental case. There is such a stigma in our society about mental illness, and I did not want to stand under that bozo arrow. But my OCD was so bad that I surrendered and gave trying various medications a shot.

Dr. Kalb explained that finding the right medication in the right dosage might take some time. It probably wasn't going to happen overnight. But medication combined with cognitive therapy could make a real difference for me. The medication would increase my levels of serotonin. If this could help, I thought, why not?

I anticipated Monkey's game of "find the perfect dress" up ahead; I saw the potential for him to make this experience a miserable maze for me. I could picture myself running around the Bay Area, trying and retrying on dresses in search of the "perfect" one. Making store clerks nuts while I compared every detail down to each independent sequin, zipper, and neckline and then do it all over again. Then at night, I would see all of the dresses in a lineup before my eyes while I was trying to sleep. Monkey would have fun asking me, "Is it this one, or is it this one?" I would wrestle with myself as I tossed and turned, chewing it all over and over again.

I worked out a deal with myself. I would allow myself three dresses to try on and to select the final dress from. Of course, I could have been obsessive in finding the three to try on, but I wasn't. I told myself that if I gave the dress an "A," then that's perfect enough. I tried on only two dresses in one shop and found it. I almost couldn't believe how well that went. I felt really good about my selection. The dress I chose was cream-colored, off the shoulders, and decorated with a lot of beading and sparkle. It cinched nicely at my waist and had an old-fashioned look to it.

I also told myself that there would be no crazy dieting. I made a deal with myself that I would eat good portions of food, and I would not overindulge. Which felt more than fair.

So far, so good. I felt in charge. For the first time, I felt as though I had Monkey on a leash and not the other way around.

I prepared for the wedding in many ways. I knew that I was doing it all right. I bought simple, satin, cream shoes in a size 9 1/2, the size that I always wore even though my foot size was only an 8. Not liking restriction is in the fiber of my OCD being. During this time, I remembered when I was five years old, begging my mom to take the elastic out of the wrists of my nightgowns and pajamas. The wrist areas were always droopy without the added elastic and tight ruffle. But looseness felt right for me.

I chose not to have my dad walk me down the aisle to give me away. I was making a clear decision for two reasons. First, my brothers Brian and Kent were the guys who had been there for me during most of the days of my life, not him. It would be a charade to have my father give me away, and I did not want false representation at my wedding. Second, with such a responsibility, he likely would have buckled, done drugs to try to handle his stress, or just not shown up altogether. Instead, I asked him if he would like to do a reading and he declined. Also in preparation for the big day, I spent hours at the high-end makeup counter at Macy's in Walnut Creek. I learned about proper eyeliner application. I even bought a book on applying makeup and read it thoroughly. My hair was colored a shiny, dark auburn, and I selected complementary colors and hues right down to the lipstick. This was the day that I was going to pull my whole look together. My day to be perfect.

I knew what I was doing. I was going about all of this correctly and with minimum stress. I was a perfect planner, and I spotted the potholes ahead of time:

Wedding location, check.

Wedding dress, check.

Wedding shoes, check.

Wedding makeup, check.

I thought ahead as to how all my makeup would be carefully transported and ready for me to use. I bought a small toolbox and had everything laid out perfectly for the special day. I even had a talk with my mom and shared with her that when she is anxious, I feel her energy and I become anxious. I asked her to please try hard to not be anxious on my wedding day.

It finally arrived, the big day! I was calm, centered, and focused mainly because I knew I was marrying my best friend. I worked very hard to keep myself steady. I was active in getting ahead of Monkey and had blocked his normal paths. I was watching myself and being in the moment, not getting swept up in any of Monkey's come-ons. Sleeping through the night and waking up early, but not too early. Coffee, but not too much coffee. I was keeping a close eye on my OCD as well. When I started to tap out a number on my jeans, I would think to myself, *I don't want to be tapping.* I was being very mindful. When I started counting calories in my head, I would think, *I don't want to be counting calories.* I seemed to have good control. I was both impressed and amazed by this. All that I had learned and practiced was working.

It was an ideal July day—sunny, not too hot, just very pleasant with a soft breeze. I could not have asked for better. I selected my mom as my maid of honor; she has always been the main lady in my life and it just seemed to make the most sense to me in my mind and heart alike. She was the woman that I was closest to and had the biggest importance. Although we went through challenging times, our love for one another was always pure and, even in the darkest hours, somehow still radiant. Liz, Doug's sister, and Nicole, my sister, were the flower girls. They were a lot older than most flower girls, but this was the way that we wanted to incorporate them into the ceremony. They both wore long, flowing lavender dresses that they picked out (I didn't want the dresses to be identical; I wanted them to style themselves and have some freedom to do so), and before and after the ceremony they tossed cream-colored rose petals.

We arrived at the Danada House early. We had more than two hours to get ready, and we headed upstairs to a large preparation room: my mom, Phyllis (Doug's mother), Nicole and Liz (our sisters), and Karen (my longtime friend who was to do my hair). The room was open with all-wood floors, large windows, and antiques placed about. I sat in front of a big antique mirror. I was in my jeans and comfy T-shirt while Karen started on my hair. My thought was to put on the dress after my hair was ready.

I was confident that she would make my hair lovely. Besides being a stylist, she was a friend and what I would imagine a big sister would be like because she gave advice. She and I discussed my hair, and we were going for a retro 1910s–1920s vintage Gibson Girl look with swoops making an updo. Karen started the process, brushing, curling, swirling, and building a masterpiece. I relaxed into it, allowing however long it took to get my hair just right.

I had commissioned an artist in the Bay Area to create hair sticks for me, and I gave these to Karen. Sterling silver pins with crystals, some ovals, some circles dangling off the end of each one, tucked into the auburn red curls and swirls, each one ready to catch the sunlight. I really had thought of everything: the crystals, my makeup, hair, shoes, dress. I was enjoying being so relaxed and prepared. I was open to being relaxed and really getting into it. It felt so peaceful that Monkey was not at the wheel.

Completely taken by my calmness, I was unaware of how much time had gone by. None of us were watching the clock. Time evaporated.

The music started playing outside. I could hear it through the open window, and it was lovely. A string trio: cello, violin, and harp. Out of the clear blue, my mom said, "The music's playing; you have to get outside now."

"What, Mom?" I was not certain that I'd heard her correctly.

"Kirsten, you need to get outside; it's time, all the people are waiting."

This new reality cut through me like a sharp knife filleting a fish from top to bottom. The calm of the room disintegrated so fast I could not hold on to it.

Way too quickly, I spiked to a new level of anxiety that I had never felt before. I felt as if I had taken two hard punches in the boxing ring. My face smeared by each glove, head and neck thrown back hard, my body thrown against the wall. My heart was pounding so hard that my face was pounding with it. Little tears came out to line the bottom of my eyelashes. I was breathing in but forgetting to breathe out. From the walls of the room came invisible piranhas biting me all over with their spiky teeth. I was experiencing unexpected full-on anxiety.

This seemed like the meanest joke that had ever been played on me.

My voice was shakier than it had ever been. "Maaaaahhhhhm, how much time do you think I have? How long before people start getting mad at meeeeeeehhhhhhhh?"

"You can have ten minutes, and that's pushing it."

I thought to myself, *I cannot possibly apply all my makeup and get my dress on in ten minutes.* I knew that watery eyes were the kiss of death for mascara. I told myself, *Stop crying! Stop crying! Do this! Get it together!* I opened my makeup kit, and it looked very sparse, nothing like how I had prepared it. At least half of my items were missing. "Mmmmmmmmmmmmmom, where is all my makeup?"

Very matter-of-factly, she said, "Oh, it opened up in the trunk of my car and some items fell out. It was too dark in there for me to see where everything was. I brought what I could."

I quickly inventoried what was in there and dove into submarine mode—the mode where I sink into myself so I can just function robot-like. Some major items were missing, like eye shadow and lip gloss. My disappointment punched me in the gut and the face. I was deeply mad at her and felt let down, but I didn't have time for any of that.

Seriously, I winced inside and asked myself, *how the fuck am I going to do this?!* I started applying under-eye concealer; thank God I had some-thing to cover the purple under my eyes, another heredity mishap. I was shaking and trembling. I told myself, *Stop crying!*

With my left hand, I tightly held my right wrist in place so I could use the black mascara to brush over my lashes without jamming the black goop into my eye and smearing it all over my face and making the situation worse. I got a swipe of mascara onto my lashes.

I knew that I had a very limited time to get everything done. There was no blush or eye shadow. I did have my dark lipstick, and I quickly swiped that over my lips. I patted light powder all over my face. It was difficult to put my dress on, but I did it. I felt that I looked like a Victo-rian ghost with a tower of amazing hair.

Just then I heard my mom blurt out, "God damn those dry cleaners!" She had ripped the sleeve of her sheer purple top. She started stomping around looking for a needle and thread. This gush of her negativity and strain surged at me and took over. I dodged into the ladies' room to get a moment to myself.

I dropped onto the floor. I was facedown on the cold tile. Enter Monkey. Of course. He started in with the taunts, telling me that a coworker of mine was going to kill me. "You think you've got trouble now; this is nothing! You will be killed by Mary!" I hit my fist to the floor. All I could see in front of me was what Monkey was providing. Frightening images of Mary standing over me holding a knife, lunging toward me, and making stabbing gestures. *Mary is going to kill me!* Intrusive thoughts kept firing at a machine-gun pace.

The researchers found that the students consistently rated the statements that were repeated as more true and valid every time they were repeated. It is known as repetition and the illusion-of-truth.

—BEN PARR, *CAPTIVOLOGY*

Usually, Monkey's repetition made things seem more truthful. Now his unrelenting repetition made it very clear to me that *it was my OCD talking!*

I started chanting, "Oh my God! Oh my God! Kirsten, you have got to get it together!"

But Monkey kept at it. In his sinister voice, teasing and tormenting again and again: "Mary is going to kill you." And he said that like he was doing me some kind of favor by giving me the information!

I tried with all my might to just touch the cold tile floor with the palms of my hands and fingers and focus my eyes on the tile and not look at the images of Mary stabbing me. Then I said out loud to myself my learned and practiced steps. "This is OCD! **R**eattribute: Chemicals are misfiring in my brain. **R**efocus: I am going to do something else. **R**evalue: This is just OCD! This is just Monkey. Goddamn it, motherfuckinggoddamnsonofabitchasshole! Fuuuuuuuuuuuuuuuuuuuuck!" I pounded my fist on the cold tiles. "I do not have time for this bullshit! Enough is enough!"

Just then, a much softer and sweeter voice came out of me. *Get up, get up!* It's as though I was having an out-of-body experience. I was like an observer, looking at the trouble I was in. I was above, coaching myself in the boxing ring. I was there to encourage, dry off my sweat, and give myself some smelling salts. *Get up, get up!* It was no longer just me and Monkey. I felt my angels close; they were standing by, watching me with profound hopefulness and belief in me.

Through my madness I was still able to feel my desire to marry Doug pumping in my heart. I asked myself, *What would someone without OCD do?* And I answered, *They'd get up and go get married.*

I wanted to be *that* person. My love for Doug and desire to be with him were stronger than my desire to please Monkey and listen to his battery-acid-like sermon. Love is stronger than Monkey. I could finally hold on to this thought. *Yes, Monkey, you are right; I will be killed by Mary, but I am pressing on anyway!* I was risking the dreaded experience and getting myself out there.

While swallowing, I tried to suck all of my tears back into my eyes and face. Although I was there on the floor, I was also in a newfound spot within myself. I was focused like I had never been before. I was floating in the middle of anger and passion. I felt decisive. I stood up erect like a Viking warrior wearing an elaborate wedding dress, hands dropped to my sides, facing forward toward the door. My racing heart had to catch up with me; composure became the name of the game. I opened the door.

Step one: a quick look at myself in the ornate mirror before me on the wall. I was still a Victorian white-faced ghost. But this was the look that I had to go with. Step two: get my wedding dress zipped up. I started to ask my mom and Karen if I looked okay, but I could feel that just asking this question and waiting for their approval were bringing more hurt to the experience. So back to Viking warrior mode. *You can do this, Kirsten.* I had to go forward and get my ass outside!

Lastly, I thought I would swipe some lip gloss over my dry lips. I looked in the toolbox and there was none in there. "Mom, do you have any lip gloss or Chapstick?"

"I have bacitracin."

I knew that, although entirely gross, the medical ointment would shine up my lips and give this Victorian ghost some much-needed life.

Well, it was no longer about me getting it together and being ready; it was about getting outside and meeting up with Doug, my best friend. I didn't want him to wait another minute for me or me for him. I went for what I really valued and did not let Monkey take any more away.

Basically what I learned is that if you're willing to take the hit of unwanted anxiety, you can continue to move in the direction that you value. And I was doing it—another notch in my courage belt!

"Mary is going to kill you!" Monkey shrieked, one last pathetic time.

I know, but I need to get married first.

It was showtime. I felt as though my mind was out of my body, carefully watching the Victorian ghost walking down the stairs. Oh, how I wished all this was better. I knew the answer, *This is what it is, and we walk forward.*

As soon as I got to the big, wide-open doors leading outside, I saw the sun shining bright and could hear the string trio playing away. My two brothers, Kent and Brian, were there, looking so handsome in their black tuxedos. They were there to walk me down the aisle of green well-manicured grass and lead me to Doug. I looped my left arm in Brian's right and my right arm in Kent's left.

I could feel that Brian and Kent were very present. When they surface their best selves, they are like knights in shining armor. They had a job to do, and it was to get their little sister down the aisle.

Joshua, my youngest brother, was also in the mix: he was walking behind us trying to keep an eye on the dress. (The dress-train straightener part was kind of accidental; I just wanted him to be a part of the ceremony.) I felt so proud to be with my three brothers. All I had for them was pure love and adoration.

There were people seated on either side, and we walked through the open middle. All of the guests looked so nice in their summer dress clothes, sitting on the white folding party chairs. I even saw summer hats with ribbons. They were here for us, for this time, for this space, for this moment, for this experience.

I felt a little bit of pure unadulterated joy. I thought to myself, *If I can just get to Doug, I will be okay. Keep moving forward.* Doug was up ahead with the minister. He was wearing his cream-colored tux and looked so dignified, handsome, and angelic in such a beautiful setting out by the pond.

Finally, I reached him, my best friend, my safe place to land.

Doug looked me in the eyes and greeted me with a big smile, dimples and all. Doug's nephew Jimmy once said, "Uncle Doug has movie star teeth." It's true, when Doug is smiling at you, it is something special. Well, there I was. I finally made it to Doug. The first thing I heard was Walter, my soon-to-be-father-in-law, say, "Oh, look, the Bride of Frankenstein." Luckily, my brain jumped over his comment like a pommel horse. No more stress could come in today. Stress and unkind words were not welcome. I was a Viking warrior and pale-faced Victorian ghost, and no one was going to mess with this moment.

My two older brothers gave me a kiss on the cheek and went to their seats next to their wives. Joshua gave me a sweet look and a smile and went to his seat as well.

Doug's mom came next; I had never seen her look prettier. Put together and confident, she flashed an enchanting smile. My mom proudly stood next to me as my maid of honor. She held her head high, and she looked stunning in her lavender dress and her matching flowy hat, a real class act. There was no sign at all that the "goddamn dry cleaners" had fucked up so royally.

I leaned in toward Doug and whispered in his ear, "I am so stressed right now, I am just trying to hang on, and I have bacitracin on my lips." (I know "I love you" would have been the thing to say.) Even though he didn't have the details of the recent situation, he seemed to understand that it had been stressful for me. Then I said, "You look great, Doug. I love you." "You look beautiful, Kirsten. I love you." Monkey stood on the outside, not allowed to get in on this moment.

Doug and I connected loosely by the hands and wrists, and we moved them together like propellers, relieving our shared stress of being up in front of everybody who meant something to us. We did this through most of the ceremony. Somehow all the stress was flowing through our hands and wrists as they circled each other. This motion was bringing comfort. It almost looked like a kid's game. However, kids would do it as fast as they could until they broke the movement and laughed. We just kept our motion going at the same pace as we stood together, visually showing the bond between us. Since the first day I met him and he reminded me of the Professor from *Gilligan's Island*.

My feet were firmly planted, figuratively and literally, because my cream-colored satin wedge heels had sunken a bit into the moist soil (I didn't let that bother me). My spiritual buzzing and discomfort faded and, deep down, just standing next to Doug made me feel better and it always had. I got to pause, stop, and be present. My mind was my own when we said our vows, looking directly into each other's eyes; this was our space. To conclude the ceremony, Amanda, Karen's daughter, whom I used to babysit, came up to the front with all of us.

While she did that, my brothers passed out little white boxes to all the attendees sitting patiently in their chairs. Kelly read a short poem I had written about love being like freedom. There it was—my passion for freedom.

I had heard somewhere that you could grow butterflies, that a company would send you little boxes with caterpillars or pupae in them. The instructions said to keep the boxes in a dark place, which I selected with my mom's consent—the closet in my old bedroom. After a short period of time, after they had been left alone in the dark, they would grow into butterflies. Kelly instructed everyone to open their boxes at the same time. One, two, three, and open! To everyone's surprise, when the boxes were opened butterflies flew out of their restrictive paper cages and into the sunlight and the bright and varied flowers that surrounded the pond.

The remainder of the wedding was glorious—and our guests seemed to agree.

Doug and I had selected a portrait photographer to take our pictures based on his amazing portfolio of still shots. We learned on our wedding day that to create these amazing portrait shots took a long time of remaining perfectly still and sort of frozen, really. I wished we could have just wrapped it up with that guy and said screw the el supremo pictures and gotten our butts inside with our family and friends.

One drama was that my mom had arranged for my dad to sit with everyone at the head of the table, but he declined, claiming that the music was too loud there. (He can only tolerate comfort.) It was hard not to take note of the empty chair she intended for him. My mom was baffled and hurt that he didn't want to be a part of the wedding party and take her up on her gracious invitation. That's my dad.

My mother's husband, Richard, whom I had also asked to do a reading, stood up and literally pulled out a tacky greeting card (probably from a nearby grocery store) and read it out loud. He was known to always write nice and encouraging speeches at other family gatherings. Was he being mean? Was he being funny? Whatever.

Here I was with Doug, my new husband, and all my friends and family (except my dad) in this beautiful setting. Everything seemed so right, and I'd made it through. Several times my sister Nicole (my dad had married one of his girlfriends and had both Nicole and Joshua) and sister-in-law, Liz, tried gossiping to me that my dad was doing drugs in the bathroom, as if informing me of the latest scandal. But I was present enough to say, "Guys, I don't care what he is doing. Please don't tell me anymore."

I think now of the Polish proverb that says, "Not my circus, not my monkey." I just didn't have it in me to worry about my dad. Much as I would have liked him to be present with me on this special day, I could see that he just couldn't be. Sometimes you have to let go of one thing so you can step forward.

Doug and I had taken swing dancing classes back in California for our special dance at the wedding. The problem was that we had never practiced. There was a lot of tugging and pulling on the dance floor with low mutterings of "This way!" and "No, this way!"

I then started a conga line and soon had more than fifty people snaking their way all over the Danada House. I even led them into the men's bathroom for an added thrill. The dancing felt so good. For added amusement I pounded on the men's bathroom stall doors and so did the conga line behind me. It occurred to me that my dad was probably in one of the stalls getting high, but I didn't care. Perhaps I was subconsciously pounding out the hurt that had built up from my relationship with my dad over the years.

Eventually, things wound down. When the vintage car pulled up out front for us, we jumped into the backseat and waved good-bye to everyone with big smiles on our faces. I pushed through my OCD and got to a better place. We were married, damn it, and I'd (we'd) made it through. Amazing.

ALL TANGLED UP, NOT THIS TIME, MONKEY

I'M NOT FLYING AROUND

YOUR STICKY SPACES

FLYPAPER CAREFULLY ARRANGED

TO CATCH THE SOUL AND DRAIN THE HEART

I'M NOT GETTING TANGLED UP IN YOUR MESSY MIND

VINES THAT SQUEEZE THE PSYCHE

TURNING BRIGHT RED BLOOD TO BLACK

YOU SADDLE UP A BUTTERFLY

AND RIDE IT 'TIL IT'S DEAD

CIRCUS OF BROKEN PIECES

BE LEFT INSIDE YOUR HEAD

A Special Blend of Wedding Jitters

· · · · · · · ·

KEY POINTS TO REMEMBER

· · · · · · · ·

When I was in the deepest throes of OCD, I could not have gotten married. So many things seemed out of reach and unimaginable. What does OCD keep you from doing?

Weddings can equal high stress. Plus, keep in mind that *Monkey loves a savory selection*—the more potential stress spots, the better he can operate.

I thought that I had planned for everything. I made all the arrangements. I had the best-laid plans. It was unbelievable. I was quietly sneaking by Monkey, and I seemed to be sneaking the whole wedding by him. No matter how much I prepared, doing my homework and knowing my steps, though, Monkey was clever and found his way in. The point is to not give up.

I found that love was Monkey's kryptonite, and love got me off the floor on my wedding day. I think love can move mountains, and come to think of it, maybe it did. My angels were right there with me. I felt a certain amount of safety knowing that they were so near.

Here's what I learned:

Seeing Monkey's game clearly is like developing an art form—it helps if your eyes are wide open. Just because you see the bait doesn't mean you have to take it. Remember, the more you do something, the better you get.

I saw that my mission was to keep developing a passion for freedom. Let determination be your fuel! Don't give up. Make note of your progress! Even the littlest accomplishments add up!

Values Clarification: Do what is important to you. Doug and I becoming engaged was what I valued; it's where my heart was. Even though Monkey threw many curveballs our way, we still managed to do what we set out to do. We rose to the occasion and didn't let Monkey stop us from getting married or completely take over the show. Monkey may toss marbles under your feet because he's a son of a gun, but you can learn how to dance, even with some pesky marbles.

Sometimes when you step forward, you have to leave something behind. Sorry, Monkey, I am finding real ways to leave the OCD Circus.

Because Doug doesn't have OCD, it is a very good and constant reminder of what someone without OCD would do and what someone without OCD does in various situations. He is like a role model in many ways. He also has learned about OCD with me and doesn't participate anymore in reassurance (OCD's love drug!). He helps me call out OCD on the spot. It is very helpful to recognize and catch OCD at the onset. So much so that I have dedicated a section of this book to exactly that concept.

· 6 ·

DANCING SHOES

A MESSAGE TO THE BOYS
How To Be Champ
LIVE CLEAN — WORK HARD — DON'T SMOKE
GET ALL THE EDUCATION YOU CAN
IF YOU DO THIS, "YOU CAN'T MISS"

Jack Dempsey

The One-Two Punch

After the wedding, Dr. Kalb and I tried a variety of medications in a variety of dosages. They were all SSRIs and their purpose was to help balance serotonin levels. During this learning period, I found out that low levels of serotonin can cause depression. No flipping wonder I sludged my way through life for so many years! (Had I only known!) My serotonin was way out of whack. Yes, I fully admit my decisions and life choices didn't help the matter!

This medication trial time was challenging. Unfortunately, it's not a one-size-fits-all sort of thing, like I had really hoped it was, but I stuck with it nonetheless.

One time I called Dr. Kalb from my cubicle because I felt as if I was going to jump out of my skin and go flying into someone else's cube. My anxiety was spiking. My words went something like this, as I gripped my desk and just about crushed the phone in my hand: "Get me off this medicine now! It's not working!" I don't think I even said hello.

After a month or two, we found something that worked for me. Once we found something that worked, I quickly started to see improvements in myself and my condition overall. Just like in life, some days were better than others. My OCD would wax and wane just like the doctor said it would.

For me, medicine did not solve the problem, but as Doug so nicely put it, medicine gave me two boxing gloves to fight with instead of just one.

I also had to develop my mental palate to discern between OCD fear and real fear, and this is a skill you can develop, too. (You can do this more and more as you become mentally healthier. It's like an art form, and it is incredibly worth the effort to begin discerning between the two fears.)

What Is Going on in My Brain?

The brains of OCD sufferers are characterized by communication problems between its deeper structures and its front part. Serotonin is a naturally occurring chemical that helps messages get from one brain cell to the next. The precise role of serotonin in OCD is not known. What is known is that OCD sufferers tend to have lower levels of it. Medications called selective serotonin reuptake inhibitors (SSRIs) prevent serotonin from getting reabsorbed by the brain cells, so it is more available to do its job. There are other ways to increase the presence of serotonin aside from taking medication. Exercise is one example.

It's not smart or even possible to throw all fear out the window in one fell swoop. It's like the old saying, "Don't throw the baby out with the bath water." Fear can be an excellent survival mechanism. Like Gavin de Becker says in his book *The Gift of Fear*, "Since fear is so central to our human experience, it is important to understand when it is a gift—and when it is a curse" (p. 11). True fear is part of our fight-or-flight wiring, and it's there for a very good reason—to protect us from harm and get us and others out of real danger.

True fear, de Becker clarifies, is a signal that sounds only in the presence of real danger; however, when you have OCD, your fear center is broken and your brain is misfiring. You're experiencing factual biochemical anxiety just as you would in "real danger." What I am talking about here is that it's a real physiological brain thing, and it's not your fault. It's what makes us unique. Other people have other challenges and things to deal with, and our broken fear center just happens to be ours.

OCD fear, on the other side of the spectrum, often works against the individual experiencing it and those around them. It can cause real debilitation and have a paralyzing effect.

Fear is where OCD gets all its momentum, and fear is how OCD manipulates us. If you are kept afraid, you are kept submissive. The feelings of fear are a big part of why those of us with OCD do what we do. So, it sounds like a conundrum, but it's not really.

One of the keys I found was to have faith in myself, not just filter ALL MY DATA through OCD. If anyone knows and can recognize your OCD at the door, it is YOU, and throughout this book we will dive into just how to do that more deeply. You can do this much better when you stay present and aware, which are skills that you can develop. What I am speaking of here is mindfulness, and we will learn more about that, too, and its importance.

I have found that the best way to identify or begin understanding whether fear is real or not is to **consider its source**. Is it coming from OCD? Or is it coming from your gut feelings and intuition? Staying in tune with yourself, "in the moment," will make your job of being a *fear traffic guard* easier.

Parasailing with the Sharks

Doug and I decided that one of the things we would do on our honeymoon in Hawaii was go parasailing, and there I was, way up high over the ocean all by myself. I felt like I could touch the clouds; I was actually passing through some small ones. The only thing that connected me to the boat below was a very long line that looked like just thick string. Doug and the captain were like little dots down below. The dark blue water went on forever with no visible edges.

At this moment, something sort of new was happening: I wasn't in the mental **"chew"** of OCD and a million and one distractions.

OCD always offered something to mentally gnaw on, sort of like a pacifier to a baby. With OCD, my mind always had something to chew on, and that could be a great distraction. OCD or not, we all do it; it's just that with OCD you can't stop the chewing. Monkey could take me out of all kinds of moments both good and bad. He was a thief—and a powerful one at that.

But here I was, up with the clouds, right here, right now. The OCD buffer was gone. I was really in the moment! There was no OCD trance, no chew.

It was all me! That crystal clear moment has stayed with me. I wasn't counting calories or obsessing about a Killing Bible, black hefty bags, my imperfections, and serial killers. I was experiencing "being here." Frankly, the thought of being rid of my OCD was scary as hell, but so, so freeing. Freeing! Now that's a feeling that I had been longing for forever.

I felt alive—more alive than I ever had on the Zipper at the amusement park. In fact, lo and behold, I learned up there on the parasail that I might actually be afraid of heights and that I don't care for floating like a balloon over the ocean! That was a brand-new feeling . . . and a non-OCD one!

Let's Dig a Little Deeper

OCD is the dean of Mind Fuck University, but I have great news for you! You don't need to be enrolled there anymore! Can we get a hoot! Hoot! High five, low five.

Let's take the next step and **Decrown, Dethrone,** and **Defrock** your OCD.

I am an OCD veteran, and it brings me enormous pleasure to share with you another way that I learned to take my Monkey down! The steps offered in *Brain Lock* are excellent, and they saved my ass at a critical time in my life. Here, I offer another way of navigating your OCD territory. Another set of tools for your OCD toolbox.

You'll learn ways to *not do what your OCD wants you to do*, stand up to him, and finally get the peace that you so deserve. Keep reading, and I will reveal some of OCD's biggest secrets of all time and expose the "Great Oz behind the curtain."

At first, it might seem really weird and possibly wrong to shine a flashlight at Monkey or your OCD (I have even felt moments of mourning and a sense of loss as I sent Monkey down the river), but it is necessary for getting onto the wellness path. One of the best things that you can do is learn about your OCD, your version of Monkey! It may seem as though you're learning to understand a foreign language. However, learning about your OCD is a great step on your wellness path.

Maybe you should get a pen or pencil and fill in the lines provided for *your* Monkey. That image makes sense for me; however, you can substitute whatever word describes what is troubling you. If *Monkey* works for you, use it; if not, make up something that does. Include a mental picture of the image you chose to represent your OCD. Have that image in the forefront of your mind. This will help you recognize and identify it from both close up and far away when it comes by for a visit.

Monkey or _____
Kung Fu; It's Not OCD,
It's YCD = Yes Can Do!

OCD is always fishing for you, putting out worm after worm, but only delivering the hook! At first, I thought that I should blast Monkey with a machine gun, like he had been blasting me for so many years. My thoughts on Monkey/OCD at this time were, *I cannot destroy him and obliterate him; however, I will not let him destroy me,* and of this I was certain.

My friend, it's time to change your pattern and begin the dance. The first thing you have to do is be open to the idea. That's it! Simple.

OCD is like a boa constrictor, limiting your freedom. It's time for you to dance your way out of its constriction.

By no means am I the Fred Astaire or Gene Kelly of OCD, but I hold my own on the dance floor and so will you. The more you practice these new dance moves, the better you'll get, and your confidence will begin to grow! OCD hates it when you have self-confidence; it's her kryptonite.

You *can* get back to a world that is not filled with [*your OCD's name here*]'s demands and orders. No more diving into the numerous tasks she has for you. You'll learn how to say, "No! Not this time, [*ditto*]! I'm the one in charge! Not you, [*and again*]! Not you!"

What You Need to Know about Your Dance Partner

If you wish to change something, the first thing you have to do is to see it the way that it is.

—BHANTE HENEPOLA GUNARATANA, *MINDFULNESS IN PLAIN ENGLISH*

Spot and identify _____ at the onset.

For me, if it looks like a Monkey, acts like a Monkey, and smells like a Monkey, it's a Monkey. My Monkey smells like bull crap! Sometimes he comes carrying roses, trying to hide his smell. But over the years, my nose got more keen, and now I can smell Monkey, roses or not, from miles away. You'll learn how to do the same thing!

Recognizing _____ at the onset is critical. OCD comes wearing different disguises, so it is important to always have your mental flashlight with you so that you can catch him or her before the damage begins—in other words, *before you take the worm.*

How Many of These OCD Traits Are Familiar to You?

You might find it helpful to put a check mark by all of the following traits that you can relate to.

❏ _____ is clever and operates with "truth nuggets." She starts with an ounce of truth to work with because the best lies carry an element of truth. (She begins with what she knows will work to reel you in. It is with a little bit of truth that she weaves her brilliant tapestry of lies and, frankly, utter bullshit—for example, cleanliness is good, having white socks is good, not getting sick is good, protecting your loved ones is good, being accepted and loved by God is good.) **Your OCD is custom-made to work on you, and your _OCD knows the truth nugget(s) you'll react to._** This is how OCD gets a real good piece of meat for you in your trap (worm on the hook!). Monkey knows your specific entry points.

❑ _____ creates thoughts and scenarios that are not true.

❑ _____ sets the trap, is an alarmist, and *will do whatever it takes to get your attention.*

❑ _____ is a markswoman. *She has extraordinary precision and knows what exactly will bring you unbridled anxiety.*

❑ _____ is an inventor that complicates things, is a noisemaker, motivates with fear, is a trance zealot, is a chatter-box always wanting to talk with you, is mean, and is an expert storyteller. Her stories are compelling! They are told as factual, and yet they are only fiction.

❑ _____ is a skilled mail carrier. She is always ready with a special delivery just for you. Just because she puts a package in your mailbox does not mean that you have to take it out and open it. Leave the package there.

❑ _____ creates entanglement. You try to make a straight line, and she turns it back into a scribble.

❑ _____ acts like she has a monopoly on the truth, is a master of disguises so she can trick you into playing along, and she owns and operates a fear factory.

❑ _____ gives you intrusive thoughts.

❑ _____ perpetuates herself.

❑ _____ wants obedience.

❑ _____ calls you names. For example, my Monkey loves to call me a fucking idiot.

❑ _____ is an inventor.

❑ _____ is like an advertisement for a good cold medicine; she promises relief.

❑ _____ is a matador and wants to get your attention.

❑ _____ is a sociopath and only thinks about servicing herself while disregarding your pain.

❑ _____ waves a rag in front of your face. She hopes that you'll grab hold of it like a dog. Don't clamp down on it. Observe it and say, "Look, there is _____, up to her old tricks." Do not take the rag in front of your face; it will only lead to more misery. Instead, deal with the discomfort of not grabbing the rag and doing her tasks.

❑ _____ gives you unanswerable questions. I call them *riddles*, which I also call *head fuck*, which in turn I call OCD's *main assignment.*

❑ _____ is not about harmony. She is about strife and conflict, about stoking the fire and keeping it going.

❑ _____ tries to suck you in. I like to call it _____ *trance.* (I almost called this book *Monkey Trance.*) She mistakenly thinks that putting you under her spell is her job.

❑ _____ does "fear casting" about catastrophic future events. Fear casting is her brand of radio.

❑ _____ broadcasts from "nonsense" radio. She has a big microphone and hopes that you tune in all the time.

❑ _____ grabs a thought, finds an entry point, and says, "Let's freak out!" It is random and it is powerful. She picks the topic and sounds the alarms (causing fear and anxiety, both big motivators).

❑ _____ is a salesperson and starts the dialogue by asking you questions or giving you something to do. She piques your interest. Once she has your interest, she is back in, and the game is on.

❏ _____ is a marketing mogul. She knows just how to present information so you buy it.

❏ _____ is a seducer.

❏ _____ is a skilled movie director. Her specialty is "mental movie making." Every camera angle, every sound effect, and every edit is made especially for you. She is very skilled and makes compelling and horrific propaganda-filled movies to motivate you into doing your compulsions. Her specialty is barraging you with constant frightening images.

❏ _____ is a validator and validates your obsessions.

❏ _____ is a toxic personality.

❏ _____ is the master of illusion and delusion.

❏ _____ is the persecutor, judge, and jury.

❏ _____ is an imaginative son of a gun.

❏ _____ makes you fearful of things yet to come.

❏ _____ tries to get you to fixate on things.

❏ _____ is the master craftswoman of illusion and delusion.

❏ _____ will taunt you with what ifs if you don't do your compulsions. What ifs have the power of suggestion and get you thinking in the wrong direction.

What Monkey or _____Wants

❏ _____ wants to be the driver and put you in the sidecar.

❏ _____ wants to hypnotize you with her pocket watch. Once you are in your OCD trance, and under her spell, she has you.

❏ _____ wants to get your attention by flashing pictures on and off (for me like flash cards or cue cards). You will do anything to get her to stop harassing you and let up. Here's an example: If you straighten the cans correctly with the labels all facing forward, you are told the harassment will stop, a catastrophe won't happen, and you will be given peace. But doing *whatever it is* that your _____tells you to do only makes you weaker and her stronger. So don't do it!

❏ _____ wants to be your coach at the side of the boxing ring. The thing about _____, though, is that she chronically gives you bad advice and you get more hurt.

❏ _____ wants obedience and compliance and demands it.

❏ _____ is like a good cold medicine advertisement that always promises relief. Perhaps a little burst of relief comes, but it is fleeting. Your OCD will quickly jump to the next thing.

❏ _____ wants you to feel guilt, feel bad, and feel annoyed. With these feelings in play, she has a better chance of sucking you in.

- ❏ _____ wants you to feed her. You make her bigger and stronger when you do your compulsions. The outcome is backward because you think that if you do the compulsions, you will make her go away.

- ❏ _____ wants you stuck in a groove.

- ❏ _____ wants to take you off your axis, off your balance. This makes you a better target for all of her sick games.

- ❏ _____ wants to always be the first to tell you, "*This time*, it is real; this time it is not OCD." Consider the source! Repeat: Consider the source!

- ❏ _____ wants you to be engaged with her.

- ❏ _____ wants to grab your attention.

- ❏ _____ wants to take you away from joy and the real moments of life and get you caught up in a loop in your head and have you doing your compulsions.

- ❏ _____ has the ability to make the images feel very alive and electric.

- ❏ _____ holds up the sign that says in bold letters REAL DANGER. YOU MUST RESPOND. It is utter bullshit; _____ is full of shit.

- ❏ Taking the mystery out of _____ sure takes the wind out of her sails and gives you a real leg up!

Here's the truth of the matter: someone has to take the first step in the healthy direction, and that person is you! *Remember, OCD is ignorant.* Okay, I said it. Pretty brave, huh!? And it needs to be retaught, and you are going to do just that! Congratulations! Rather than dedicate your precious time to servicing your OCD, you are going to reclaim your time, reclaim your life. Now is your chance to get relentless about your freedom. Let's do this!

I'm sharing with you what I made up for myself and what has made a world of difference in my mental health and overall well-being. Are you ready and open to learning a new dance? Your dance moves will give you another superpower, and you'll get closer to your freedom. Learn the moves that I have outlined next. Instead of doing everything precisely right for your OCD, use that ability to be precise with your dance moves (I know you've got it in you). They are your chance out of OCD and OCD's intended constriction.

Here we go: there are nine Kung Fu Dance Moves that I have created. I know it sounds like a lot at first. In the beginning, your dance moves might seem and feel really choppy, but the more you practice, the smoother they'll get, and the better you'll get on the dance floor with your OCD. Eventually, you'll flow through your moves, and they will become automatic. I am living proof of this!

Address yourself by your name and your chances of acing a host of tasks, from speech making to self-advocacy, suddenly soar.

—PAMELA WEINTRAUB,
"THE VOICE OF REASONS,"
PSYCHOLOGY TODAY

Your OCD Kung Fu Dance Moves

We'll address and take our time to walk through each move. Think through these moves in chronological order in preparation for OCD's arrival. When your OCD arrives, you'll have already practiced your empowering moves and started to get into the flow of them. Lastly, when you conduct your inner monologue, or if you choose to say them each out loud (which I recommend), address yourself by your first name.

Inner language can focus thinking, enhance planning, and prevent the poison of later rumination.

—PAMELA WEINTRAUB, "THE VOICE OF REASONS," *PSYCHOLOGY TODAY*

Your name goes in front of the steps. Follow me.

Kirsten or _____, ACCEPT, "Yes, I have OCD."

Kirsten or_____, FOCUS, get mindful, aware, and present. Look forward, with the strength of a lion in your heart and don't let OCD in the door!

Kirsten or _____, IDENTIFY, spot Monkey at the onset. I see you!

*Kirsten or _____, BREATHE and **PAUSE** together; call on your inner warrior! Get your balance, pump up your chest. Gather all* *of yourself. Stay calm. Before taking action, choose your response and halt the downward spiral.*

Kirsten or _____, GREET, "Hello, my OCD." Wave to her if you want to. Better to treat it as a friend.

Kirsten or _____, STAY AWARE, I hear the alarms you are sounding, OCD; however, I won't get pulled in by your come-ons.

Kirsten or _____, AGREE and say YES to your OCD. YES, that a catastrophic thing might happen. Say YES to the anxiety that not doing your compulsion brings to you.

Kirsten or _____, REMEMBER, you are dancing with OCD, which is full of lies. You can get through the anxiety, the alarms sounding will fade, and your anxiety will pass.

Kirsten or _____, FORGIVE, your OCD is what makes you unique and still lovable.

❖ ❖ ❖ ❖ ❖ ❖ ❖

Congratulations, Kirsten or _____, you have not gone into your OCD trance! You have not done what your OCD wants you to do! You raised the bar, my friend! You are on your path to wellness! Keep in mind that just like anything else, the more you practice, the better you'll get.

_____ is in the sidecar, and that is that! She may sound alarms. Remember that this sounding off in your head is chemicals misfiring, and that's all there is to it. There is no riddle to solve. Say "_____, there is no fight. We are friends. You can scream at me all you want, but I will remain the one in charge."

Your OCD Kung Fu Dance Moves

· · · · · · · ·

KEY POINTS TO REMEMBER

· · · · · · · ·

Practice and visualize your steps!

1. Accept

2. Focus

3. Identify

4. Breathe and **Pause**

5. Greet

6. Stay Aware

7. Agree

8. Remember

9. Forgive

So you feel choppy on the dance floor do you?
Don't worry practice will get you there. Where?
Your freedom! It's worth all the effort and more.

It is at the "pause" that you redirect your mind and you get to transform and head on to your big, happy life. For me, it was where people "ate ice cream and had some fun." Where would you like to go from your pause? There are endless possibilities, and the big, wide, promising world is waiting for you! Step into it.

One Night the Phone Rang

By now I was fully on board with the fact that I had OCD. I was still doing my exposure homework (finding and creating those opportunities for myself), taking my medicine (totally by my own choice), and continuing to get better at managing my OCD by doing the Monkey Kung Fu Dance Moves. (I am ready when OCD arrives.)

Between stimulus and response there is a space.
In that space is our power to choose our response.
In our response lies our growth and freedom.

—VIKTOR E. FRANKL

I was staying late at work one evening when the phone rang at my desk. It was around 8 p.m. I almost didn't answer it, but something inside me told me that I should. It was a headhunter. She had been referred to me by someone at the toy company. [Whoever you are, THANK YOU!] She was calling about a marketing manager position in the music and video division of a large retailer in the book, video, and music industry at their corporate headquarters in Ann Arbor, Michigan, which was much closer to my family that lived in the Chicago area. Although I was grateful for the friendships that I did make at the toy company, I was thrilled to find out that after extensive interviewing I was offered the new position back in the Midwest.

However, a new job meant a new cast of characters and plotlines to work with and within. It was like entering an already-in-progress stage play and being dropped into it. There were good guys and villains, kind people, and smart, talented people; and there were sociopaths, agendas (including but not limited to hidden agendas), and always office politics—so draining! Yes, work was being done and objectives were being met, but there was always so much more beyond the surface.

In reflection, I can see clearly that sometimes I danced with the multiple personalities and egos better than I did at other times. I also had social anxiety, and sometimes the utter awkwardness I felt as Kirsten Weirdsten, especially in group settings, was hard to work through and get on top of. OCD taught me how to be a good actress, and sometimes that's how I got by.

My department in particular was a major distribution channel for the music industry at the time. We got some mighty and memorable perks. I actually got to sing on stage with Sting at his sound check in a small and intimate venue in Detroit. I fought my way through my anxiety and got my butt up there for this once-in-a-lifetime opportunity. Sure, my heart pounded, my palms got sweaty, but I powered through and I am glad that I did. It's Sting, for gosh sakes!

I've eaten dinner with Susan Olsen, the actress who played Cindy Brady, and k.d. lang; met Jessica Simpson; and even got to enjoy Rascal Flatts singing in our conference room. At another time, I attended a video industry party in Vegas (my not so favorite place). From way across the Olympic-sized pool, there he stood, Shaquille O'Neal, dressed in all white. My jaw dropped when I spotted him across all the chlorine. His two security guards standing next to him looked like tiny pipsqueaks, and I know they must have been really big guys. And there were so many more memorable encounters; meeting celebrities and artists was novel and a fun aspect of that job.

It was a few jobs later, however, that I came to the complete realization that I didn't fit in well with the corporate environment.

I felt like a root-bound plant that didn't quite fit in its container anymore and perhaps never quite did. I wanted my imagination to burst out and get some creative fresh air. In the back of my mind, I had always wanted to start and run my own business. *I longed to build the culture and set the tone*, not just arrive to it daily and exist among a cast of characters—unfortunately some doing some despicable things, including gaslighting as a hobby. I had been reporting to Monkey my whole life; I didn't want any more bosses.

· 7 ·

FINDING NUTRIENTS

A Bigger Picture

fter returning to the Midwest, I also became a proud member of the International OCD Foundation, the organization Doug had heard about on NPR all those years before. I was out of the closet now. The foundation is built on creating OCD awareness by providing information, the latest research, and help to people living with OCD and their families and loved ones. Well, actually a lot more than that, but that's the general idea. They have a terrific and inspiring newsletter with insights coming from doctors, OCD sufferers, and family members, and it was my hope to actually attend one of their annual conventions.

I started meeting with a doctor in Ann Arbor for OCD management. We met weekly on Tuesday nights.

One Tuesday before our meeting, I was at Michael's crafts store and read a flier on the wall announcing that cake decorating lessons were being offered on Tuesday nights. I have always loved baking and decorating cakes and cupcakes, but I was busy Tuesday nights with my OCD doctor. I had an appointment to keep! I saw no other way. So I left Michael's and went to see the doc.

He was particularly chatty that evening. He told me that other OCD sufferers manifest their OCD differently and have all different kinds of anxiety triggers. He said, "I want to show you something," as he rolled his chair to an oversized metal cabinet with big pullout drawers. He pulled out a toilet seat and held it up to me and said, "Look." He then proceeded to show me a whole collection of toilet seats that he had stashed away in that drawer. He took out one after the other; it was a parade of flippin' toilet seats!

He explained, "Some people with OCD cannot touch or use toilet seats and are terrified to do so. For exposure therapy purposes, I look at and touch these toilet seats with some of my other patients."

This is it, I thought to myself. *God, I am so fucking tired of OCD.*

It hit me like a ton of bricks. *I didn't want to look at toilet seats anymore!* I'm truly sorry toilet seats have some magic power over some people. That must truly suck for them. Toilet seats are usually a part of daily human life; there's no two ways around it. But I'm done! None of these OCD fears are real; they are all made up, and we buy into them. We are all completely believing an illusion.

The good news is: if you can recognize illusion as illusion, it dissolves. The recognition of illusion is also its ending. Its survival depends on you mistaking it for reality.

—BHANTE HENEPOLA GUNARATANA,
MINDFULNESS IN PLAIN ENGLISH

Eureka! I felt as if I had just struck some sort of OCD gold!

I have to get out of here, I thought. *I feel like I'm going to suffocate. My life is passing me by, and I want to grab on to it! I want to grab on to my life and let OCD fucking pass on by.*

Seeing through the peek hole, the bird in the cage sees the whole room, sees the whole vista.

—ANONYMOUS

I said to the doctor, in my nicest voice possible, "I don't want to be here anymore. I feel like I am ready to go like *right now, this second.* I'd rather be in a cake decorating class at Michael's."

He smiled and said, "That's a wonderful idea," and off I went.

From then on, my Tuesday nights became filled with some newly accessed creativity and fun-to-decorate cakes.

Bloom

To continue on my medication, which I believed was helping along with my exposure therapy—like looking at messy cords by my computer and just allowing the mess, letting them just be and not straightening them—I needed to meet with a nurse. Pam was the nurse assigned to my case. I had to check in with her, face-to-face, to receive her evaluation. *Sucks!* I thought. My OCD was so much better, and I just wanted to get on with things! I was so sick of OCD! I was sick of thinking of OCD and talking about it! I thought to myself, *Just make my Pam meetings go real fast so I can get my medicine refills and hit the road.*

No joke, when I first met her, I did have slight waves that she could be connected to a serial killer, so I thought I should probably keep things about myself very brief and not too revealing. After all, sharing information can be a gateway to a serial killer!

Recognizing my fear as OCD fear—and getting past it so I could have a healthy relationship with Pam—was one of the best things that I have ever done. I'd stared down Monkey, the fear striker, and won. Those little victories add up, you know. They will for you, too.

Pam's office was welcoming and had sort of a chill vibe. There were healthy plants, a Buddha on one of the end tables, and different collectibles that she had received from patients.

I'm doing my best to paraphrase our conversation. I can't recall it exactly word for word, but here's the gist of it.

Pam said, "Where are you at with your OCD?"

I said, "Well, I had an epiphany looking at toilet seats recently."

"Tell me about this epiphany; this sounds interesting."

"It was that I wanted to be living, not just reporting to my OCD, which by the way I call Monkey."

"I like that. Monkey seems to be fitting."

"I still struggle with my OCD, but ironically what I try to do is not struggle with it. The act of struggling only makes it stronger and me weaker. Kind of like that Chinese finger puzzle, the one that tightens up on your fingers. So instead, I work on acknowledging, accepting, and coping with my OCD; it's not always easy.

"The things I have in my OCD arsenal are knowledge, medication, tools, techniques, and a wealth of practice and a small network of family members who know I have it. The medicine is helping a lot, and I need a refill." So I thought to myself, *Okay, Pam, I gave you the lowdown; now give me the script.*

"So you're not totally free from your OCD, but you understand it a lot better."

"Yeah, OCD used to always bother me and although it still bothers me, it does bother me less. When my OCD flairs up, and I start to feel catastrophic feelings, like the house is going to burn down if I don't check the stove one more time, I tell myself that what I am experiencing is OCD. I identify it.

"Sometimes I even close my eyes and imagine myself spraying with black spray paint the letters *OCD* over what is bothering me." I said, "Identifying Monkey at the onset helps me to stay in touch with reality, instead of falling for the umpteenth time into my OCD, which I call Monkey trance."

At last, our talk was over and I got my refill.

On my way to the front desk with my new prescription in hand, Monkey jumped into the picture like Spider-Man quickly dropping into a scene, "You are so stupid! Why did you tell her so much? That was really risky, not knowing her at all. You better hope that she is not connected to a serial killer. You better watch what you share with her!"

I had many more appointments with Pam over an eleven-year period. I've laughed with Pam and cried with Pam. She and I traveled far together in her office, and I'm forever grateful. She helped me to clear space for something beyond Monkey, even beyond my own mind, into deeper awareness.

Rocket Fuel

When Doug was a boy, his best buddy was his doxie (Dachshund) named Stretch. I, on the other hand, did not have this warm connection to these dogs sometimes referred to as "hot dogs." I was always secretly afraid of them because of their unusually long backs and seemingly strange vertebrae. I always thought that having one as a pet wasn't such a great idea, in fear of them breaking their backs in half in some unfortunate accident. Sounds like OCD and irrational fear piping in, doesn't it?

Around the same time that I began meetings with Pam, I told Doug that I thought it only fair that he should have a Dachshund. I knew how badly Doug wished for a doggie and really wanted the doxie breed.

I pushed past my initial hesitation and fear, and how thankful I am that I did. From the moment that I held our doxie puppy (he's a black-and-tan), I knew that *love was locked in immediately* (something Sergeant promised so many years ago but never could deliver on). We named our little guy Rocket. When he was a puppy, he was so adorable that he even looked like a living Disney character. His eyes were round; his nose was round, and even his ears looked round. Neighborhood kids would frequently come to our front door and ask if they could play with the puppy. Rocket LOVED IT.

I've learned a lot of valuable things from Rocket. He practices "nowism"; the only place he exists is in the present moment. He has fresh eyes and is not bogged down from guilt of the past or fear of the future. He's a wonderful example of how to be present and allow yourself to experience the pure joy of each fleeting moment. Rocket connects me to pure love and to my higher power. I thank him for that, for those are some of the best connections around!

At night, his warm muzzle and whiskers are near my face, and hearing him breathe is so wonderfully calming. I have even cried into his animal fur when I have been sad, and without judgment, he has let me. I asked Rocket once if he was my OCD angel, and he licked my face. One of my genie wishes is that everyone gets to experience true love with an animal. It's soul nourishing and boundless. All of my animals have been some of my best friends, hands down. My memories of them and the time we've shared together are delightful love-filled soul fossils that really made their love mark on me, or, better put, in me.

Tune In to the Imagination Station

After several medicine updates with Pam, I started to feel safe sharing with her that I was getting back some of my mind space. I was getting back some of the 90 percent that Dr. Kalb had talked about so many moons ago. So now the question was, what do I do with it, this energy and new and welcomed available space? I needed new outlets for my creativity and imagination now that Monkey was not stealing it away nearly as much, squandering it, using it against me, and immobilizing my state of well-being anymore.

I was actively trying to not do what my OCD was telling me to do, like leave things alone. This way of being seemed so counterintuitive at times. My whole life before now I was doing what OCD was telling me to do. So in the beginning, leaving things "as is" was a brand-new approach and a very uncomfortable approach at that, but I was making it more my routine. I was getting better at letting my anxiety ride, and when Monkey was tempting me with the comfort and resolution after doing more mind riddles, I would just say, *Nope, Monkey, it doesn't matter, no matter how much you chatter! Whatever puzzle you want me to solve now, sorry bud, I am just leaving the puzzle on the table.*

I always wonder why birds stay in the same place when they can fly anywhere on the earth. Then I ask myself the same question.

—HARUN YAHYA

I always remember what Dr. Kalb shared with me, that actively practicing exposure therapy will create desensitization over time. Let me tell you, though, I did not have fun *creating* desensitization; the real fun came once I had acquired it. Desensitization is the real prize, not like the empty prize OCD leads you on with. You can imagine desensitization like this: it's like little-welcomed callouses over sensitive spots. Like a coat of armor.

Later I will share with you the biggest exposure therapy of my life. Bigger exposure therapy than what I could have ever imagined for myself.

Just as I was considering employing myself in a new way, I was also going to employ Monkey in a new way. Now that Monkey was in my sidecar (most of the time, but not all of the time), I wanted to have harmony with him, not just wrestling matches.

I knew that I needed a lot of mental activity to keep Monkey busy and my creativity thriving and us both working in the same direction. I needed an outlet that was not self-defeating. I needed to put Monkey to work, so to say. I needed to rechannel my energy including this fellow.

Having Monkey in my life, and wishing to be an optimist, I extracted some good from my relationship with him after all. I had to think of ways to put my hyper-developed OCD skills to good use. Reporting to Sergeant first and then Monkey had made some of my senses very keen, like concentration and focus, and I was able do all kinds of tasks at once. Tapping out to a certain number while taking notes in class, for example. OCD was operating on one track, and my other self was doing the outside stuff and trying to interact and navigate through the world (which was not always easy). I was definitely a mental gymnast. I knew how to make things look spot-on, because Monkey required perfection in so many of my actions. I could hunker down on something, not let up, and be goddamn tenacious. I wanted to tap into these fine-tuned abilities, but use them in a good and beneficial way.

It was time to take stock. What did I enjoy? What color was my parachute, anyway? I had always been so consumed with OCD that I never had the time to give any real thought to those things. If I didn't know better, I actually had some spring in my step, and a spark of excitement.

> **Find out what you are, and be that. Don't
> find out what you aren't and try to be that.**
>
> —DR. WAYNE W. DYER,
> *WISHES FULFILLED*

I'd had more than fifteen years of experience in the sales and marketing arena as well as product development by that point. And meanwhile Doug and I had amassed large quantities of retro "stuff." We were collectors, after all. For years we had been hitting up antique stores and estate sales; you could find us scouring and sifting the earth anywhere. Together we had acquired a much-loved collection of original vintage illustrations, and that's just the beginning. Everything from movie posters, books, magazines, advertising, point-of-purchase displays, vinyl toys, party favors, retro candy boxes, and everything in between. For instance, if it was paper from the past, and as obscure as an unused 1950s cocktail napkin with adult cartooning on it, we might have it. If it spoke to us on some level, we might have it. I even found a yellow plastic Twinkie the Kid ring from the 1970s (score!) and Cracker Jack and gumball machine toys in mint condition. No sir, these didn't get tossed in the garbage.

I thought specifically about all the intriguing art and images sitting there in flat files in Doug's art studio, never seeing the light of day, just stashed away. I yearned to give all this incredible imagery, especially our paper ephemera, a new life and bring it to the world again, possibly repurpose it in a different way. But how?

So I tossed around a couple of ideas with Doug and then landed on this: *What if I was to shrink down one of these 1930s pinup magazines and feature the miniature-sized cover art on a necklace?*

I used our copier and shrunk the art way, way down and found a metal pendant that I could use to frame it like a piece of art. Then I thought, *How about a coaster set?* And what if I took some of the great men's faces in these 1950s magazines . . . the classic guy with the buzz cut, the guy with the distinct black retro glasses . . . and gave them classic retro names like Harold or Harvey? I could have four different guys in a set and call them "Drinking Buddies." So you'd never have to drink alone.

The first thing I made was the mini magazine necklace. I had never poured clear resin before (I even wore a gas mask to not breathe in the toxic chemicals), and it was a challenge to get the hang of it. I was not a jewelry maker, but I would become one! My imagination was being rerouted, and it felt good. Standing up to Monkey took courage, but courage is cool. I like to think of courage as inner warrior juice! You have it, too! It's delicious!

The essence of you — the you who is a spiritual being having a temporary human existence — is cultivated in your imagination.

—DR. WAYNE W. DYER,
WISHES FULFILLED

I told my sister-in-law, Liz, about my ideas for a retro-inspired line of fun and functional, highly desirable products. I said that I needed to test out the market before I got too carried away. *Would other people like this stuff? Could I make some kind of job out of it?* I wondered.

She suggested going for the rockabilly crowd (the counterculture that appreciates the vibe, clothing, music, and lifestyle of the 1950s). She knew of a rockabilly music and car show taking place in Indianapolis. There'd be people selling stuff like vintage clothing and music. I thought, *Why not me? I can make and sell stuff.* I told Doug that I needed a name for my new venture, and he came up with Retro-a-go-go! I liked it immediately. From a marketing standpoint, it seemed like a good umbrella for all the things I was yet to create.

Doug was clear up front: "Stoney," he said, "I will support you with this, but I don't want to be any part of it." He was busy with his own art projects and a demanding corporate gig.

So, flying solo, I got to work making retro-inspired jewelry and coasters and reserved a vendor spot at the upcoming rockabilly event.

Liz met me in Indianapolis and helped me out—from setting up the Retro-a-go-go! goods to mingling with the customers. The show was great; we sold out of a ton of merchandise! The possibilities seemed limitless. I was where the wave meets the sand, and it was going to be quite the swim, indeed! I was excited about what was ahead and not fearful.

You're the "BIG SHOT" in my LIFE

Who's This Now?

The next time I saw Pam, I told her about Retro-a-go-go! and said that **it had to be successful or I would die!** I told her there was no way I could go back into the **corporate meat grinder!** If Retro-a-go-go! didn't work, **I would be crushed forever!**

She pointed out how I spoke in absolutes, with big words that had big meanings.

She said, "Kirsten, do you hear the language that you're using? Will you really die if you don't succeed? Would you really go into a 'meat grinder' if you had to go back into the corporate environment? Would something really come out of the sky and crush you?"

She went on to say, "Sure, you would like for Retro-a-go-go! to be successful, and that is a good goal; but if it doesn't work out, you will survive and do something else."

Pam had a way of taking me out of my world of absolutes and gently bringing me back to a more mellow and grounded reality. She encouraged me to pay attention and **listen to my inner narrator**. (Yep, we all have one, OCD or not.) I should pay attention to my *inner voice* and how I talk to myself. She went on to say that how we talk to ourselves is very important to our sense of self and self-esteem.

It seemed as if I was on the next level. I had been working diligently with my OCD management and remaining in the driver's seat of my life. Now there was something else to look out for and deal with? My inner narrator, my own mind sort of beyond OCD? This didn't sound fun.

The results of listening to my inner narrator surprised me.

One day I bought a light green sweater at Target. Backing out of my parking space, I heard a voice in my head, clear as day: *You are such an idiot! Do you know how many green tops you have already? It is so stupid to get another one. You should have gone with the fucking blue one!*

Whoa! Hold the phone!

Who was speaking to me this way? If it wasn't Monkey, then who? Me! My own head? My own mind? This just had to be the inner narrator Pam was talking about.

I'm sure the inner narrator is a blood relative, possibly a cousin of Monkey!

To see one's predicament clearly is a first step toward going beyond it.

—ECKHART TOLLE, *A NEW EARTH*

The next time I was in Pam's office I said, "I'm floored how much my inner narrator talks and says really bad and horrible things to me." I told her about what I heard at Target and at other observed times.

Pam asked, "Do you speak that insensitively and cruelly to anyone else? Do you call anyone else in your life a fucking idiot or stupid?" She then asked, "How would you have handled Target if you were in the mode of being kinder to yourself?"

I thought for a second and said, "I probably would say something like this: 'You know, Hun, it's easy to see why you would buy another light green sweater because you love that color and that is why you have so much of it. However, to add variety to your wardrobe, would you like to return this one and get the blue one instead?'"

Like I learned to speak the language of Monkey, I needed to speak *the language of my mind, or in other words, my inner narrator.* The first step was to keep observing and start being kinder to myself and have self-compassion (which I was not used to practicing at all).

But how could someone separate themselves from their inner narrator when it seemed to be their number-one messaging center? I still had much to learn!

There was life and insight in Pam's office, where everything seemed clearer, and then there was life outside of Pam's office, where it was up to me to put into action the things that I'd learned.

Before I left her office, Pam gave me this helpful list called the Checklist of Cognitive Distortions from *Feeling Good* by David D. Burns, MD. The list was fascinating. It covered everything from all-or-nothing thinking to our mental filters to discounting the positives to blame. Basically, our very own mind is capable of defeating us!

Perception and the Power to Choose

Over the years Monkey had created such a deep groove of fear, doubt, negativity, and self-defeat. It was an easy groove for my mind to slip right into, like a needle being dropped onto a record.

My work was cut out for me. I was tired enough of my pain and was dedicated to trying a new way, with a heartfelt desire to get to a better place. Basically creating a new groove in the record for that needle to drop into! Damn, navigating your own mind—this shit is like surgery! Back to wearing the white lab coat!

I didn't want another director in my head making me feel bad and unsettled. Fuck that shit!

I was learning that how we see things, hear things, and interpret things makes such a difference to our quality of life and our impact on others. Our thoughts and attitudes determine how we see the world, and we ourselves choose these very thoughts and attitudes. We choose which path to go down. I realized that if I could develop my awareness, see my mind in action *before* it took over the show (there's that pause idea again), I could possibly change and redirect it.

We each have two internal directors vying to control our movies: a love-based one that recognizes our inherent good in this very moment; and a fear or ego-based one that thrives on keeping us from knowing who we really are, largely by miring us in the past and future. *We* choose which of these dueling directors is in charge — and thereby what we see of the world — simply by choosing which of the two we invest in with our own innate free will.

—JEFF BELL, *REWIND, REPLAY, REPEAT*

I learned that I could consciously make a *swapportunity* (thank you, Yoplait, for this fun word) and go down another mental path. Instead of the path of gloom and doom, being or feeling negative and hosting pain and drama, I could *choose* to do, choose to see, things a little differently.

My eyes were wide open, and my mind was open as well. I was in the perfect place for transformation.

One Simple Dandelion

I am reminded of a time I was walking outside with a friend and saw a dandelion, the kind that is light gray and fluffy and the seeds are ready to break apart. I used to blow on these as a kid and make a wish. Anyway, I blew at all its fluffiness and said to my friend, "Oooh, make a wish!"

She said, "That's not a wish! That's a weed seed!"

It can be argued either way, but which path sounds more fun?

A Front Row Seat

There was the time I commented on my neighbor Ann's beautiful purple flowers climbing on a vine on her front porch. She responded, "Yeah, they are beautiful, but I am sad." When I asked why, she said, "They only blossom like this for two weeks of the year. I wish they stayed around longer."

How interesting, I thought. Here are these radiant flowers, and they're bringing her sadness. Now she had an opportunity to love them and cherish them that much more because they were leaving soon. Her sadness was her own choice, and she was not even realizing it. I thought they, like life, are fleeting and she had a front row seat to something beautiful *right now*. She and I were at the same place, yes; however, we saw what was before us differently.

Clear the road for
car of Spring,
laden with bright
flower and bud,
Dying winter's
requiem sing,
Pulses beat with
quickened blood!

Anxiety Sandwich

Meanwhile, Retro-a-go-go! was growing in popularity. Our product assortment was expanding, and the company was growing in leaps and bounds. We created a website, retroagogo.com, and we had a small team of people making and filling customer orders. We were selling to the end consumer and to stores across the world.

Our products were making people happy. And that made me feel good and inspired to create more! Again, that valuable spark.

I started the business at my kitchen table and then graduated to running Retro-a-go-go! from my basement. Being the face of the business meant that I had to get on the road and out of my natural habitat. My OCD doesn't like disruption!

I was on my first trip to Vegas for the business, oh boy! I bought an empty ten-by-ten-foot booth space at the Las Vegas Convention Center during a wholesale show in hopes of generating customer orders from store owners who could check out the offering firsthand. It was my big chance to display all my wares: accessories, jewelry, apparel, and home décor items (all with a retro twist and flair). Just parking there is stressful, not to mention the logistics of everything else that needs to come together.

I tried to handle it all, including all the newness, the best I could. For me, packing a suitcase, leaving the house, and taking my well-being on the road—that was a big deal. I liked my things, just *not* in a suitcase. To me, the inside of my packed suitcase looked like the nearly intolerable collect-all kitchen junk drawer, and I just wanted to organize it, organize it, and organize it, over and over and over again (yes, the mighty compulsion pattern lives!). Often my well-being hinged on outside elements, details, and variables, and with travel there were so many and I frequently felt out of control. From navigating the airport to my time in Vegas, including all the social anxiety that trade shows can stir up, travel was tough! Yes, I did it all, but every time I dreaded it like a cat going to the vet! Traveling provoked my anxiety, and that meant Monkey and my inner narrator were at the ready.

At the airport and in Vegas, there was too much stimulus and input that I was exposed to; it could really get me jacked up, from tremendous noise, loads of strangers to deal with, not to mention those just streaming by, people coming and going with all different mood levels (a super tough environment for a "puller" to succeed in). The number of foreseen and unforeseen variables and problems that got thrown at me was endless and exhausting (but my oh my, what an exposure training ground!).

Some moments I did much better than others. When I felt utterly out of control, I fell back into tapping, counting, going over calorie intake on my invisible chalkboard, blinking to certain numbers, and checking and rechecking just about everything I came in contact with. Thinking and rethinking and ruminating. Argh!

Going to Vegas wasn't little exposure challenge by little exposure challenge (which I truly would have preferred). It was exposure central. It was high anxiety all at once and for a solid week with almost no letup and very little real rest. The whole trip was not only mentally fatiguing, but also incredibly physically demanding: dragging stuff out of the storage locker (hundreds and hundreds of pounds of it) in humid 95-degree weather, driving the van around town and navigating Vegas, jumping in and out of the van, walking long distances, opening boxes, climbing on tables to get the lights set up—you get the idea. It was exhausting to get there and get set up, and the show hadn't officially opened yet to the wholesale buyers. I must not forget to mention that it's so much harder to manage OCD when you don't feel rested and balanced. To help me cope with the stress of it all, the first thing I always did when I got to Vegas was buy a pack of cigarettes and start compulsively puffing away.

My Retro-a-go-go! booth setup was always elaborate. I would try to access my decades of perfectionism—"el supremo" (to essentially work with and employ Monkey in some way) and make it—my experiences of knowing how to make things look really good—work for me instead of against me. It's a delicate balance, however, and if I wasn't paying close attention and keeping Monkey occupied, he would want back in the driver's seat. I would allow myself to get the booth 90 to 100 percent beautiful. Allowing a range (and not just 100 percent perfection in all things) gave me much-needed breathing room. OCD's basic nature is not to like or allow "ranges." Oh well, I am in charge and I do! New Captain on deck!

And then, voilà! Showtime! I had to be "on," upbeat, chatty, friendly, and informative. I had to have the right lipstick on, hair done right, clothes nice (I felt like a flight attendant really going the extra mile). This sounds "el supremo" doesn't it! Old habits are tough to break!

With hard work should come rewards, right? I felt as though it was only fair for me and whomever I brought with me on the trip to help out to be rewarded handsomely. I would look forward to the end of the very "on" day. After a long day of stress, we would have a drink or drinks; for me, the more alcohol I could throw down the hatch, the better. There were a few times when I drank myself into oblivion. I reasoned with myself that I needed help dealing with my anxiety, and cigarettes and drinking were my go-to crutches (old habits die hard!). I had this groove already in my head, and it was easy to drop right in to help me cope with stress. The mornings were extra tough because I would wear my hangover like a heavy bag of wet sand, and I would have a headache all day long.

Although challenging, and even more so because I had done myself in the night before, overall I felt like my creativity was finally nestled in the right home. I had a tremendous and artful outlet and I was thankful for that. I enjoyed being around all these other independent people doing their own thing, from my fellow artists selling their wares to the store owners walking the show. I loved some of the fun store names that I sold my products to; some of my favorites are Commander Salamander, Berserk and the Junkman's Other Daughter, and so many others.

Like in Making a Movie, Take Ten Thousand and Two!

I shared with Pam that Retro-a-go-go! and everything about it was exposure therapy to the extreme and that I did not necessarily like that part and had a difficult time coping. I felt I was getting more desensitized, bit by bit, to the onslaught of stimuli that used to derail me in no time flat. I shared with her that I would sneakily do my compulsions to try to gain some feelings of control, and drink and smoke to relieve stress. Pam could always get confessions out of me. She just blew right by the BS and got to some real issues.

On the other hand, though, I was proud to impart that there was some real growth. I shared with her that due to Retro-a-go-go!, I could now leave voicemail messages and frequently not even listen to them once before sending. I could write notes to people around the Retro Studio and even send written messages and packages out into the world without fearing what I might have written and the consequences to follow. I didn't even fear the stranger, yet possible serial killer that was going to be on the receiving end of my mail and packages. I could do all this and survive. I was sending out packages by the thousands. Another piece of confidence went into my "I can do this" satchel.

Up for Wellness!

I attended one of the International OCD Foundation's annual conferences. To my delight, people (doctors, OCD sufferers, and loved ones) weren't walking around in stuffy suits. No, not at all; everyone was really casual. I found it to be a very accepting and welcoming environment.

There were so many interesting and thoughtful classes and seminars available for people of all ages—both children and adults. Sometimes it was hard to choose one learning opportunity when there were other great ones going on at the same time.

There was something for everybody. Whatever OCD and anxiety manifestation someone was dealing with, groups of people there were dealing with the same thing. There were checkers, perfectionists, those with body dysmorphic issues and eating disorders, hoarders, and so much more. I learned about the other terribly intrusive things that some people with OCD were dealing with. I clearly saw that we may be in different battles, but we are all in the same war.

My heart connected with everyone—the sufferers and those who loved them. They too are sufferers, like Doug. OCD has longer arms and is able to hold more people hostage than just the OCD sufferer. The healthier I became, the more I could clearly see this. Also, everyone was up for wellness! There was even a room filled with books to buy on all kinds of anxiety topics and all different ways of getting help. While I was there, I bought a book called *Rewind, Replay, Repeat* by Jeff Bell (a fellow OCD sufferer on his path to wellness), and he signed it for me. That was a big deal. "For Kirsten, All things are possible when we dare to believe! Jeff Bell." He instantly became a role model.

Although it was apparent that there was tremendous suffering caused by OCD, it was also apparent that there was tremendous hope and so many caring people dealing with some horribly debilitating things.

In one of the interesting seminars that I attended, the very compassionate panel of doctors and sufferers opened the floor to anyone who had something to share with the room after they had spoken about

OCD and shared some of their own insights and knowledge. One caring mother of a son with OCD went up to the microphone. She spoke with unsureness and just a slight lilt of hopefulness in her voice. She shared that things at home were better and that her son was no longer showering for three hours a day, just two. Not only was his mind hurting, but I'm sure his skin was hurting, too. OCD is weird like that: you think you are giving yourself talcum powder and what you're really doing is giving yourself battery acid. This mom's love for her son was palpable. She was willing to stay the course and learn what she could so she could continue to help and encourage him to get on a healthier path.

I even took the microphone and said (and now looking back this seems so silly), "What if you go to the store, and when you get home, you see that one of the plums you selected is bruised and not perfect?" (My resurfaced el supremo—perfectionism—thinking took the floor!) The panelist who responded said, "If I had a bad plum, I would toss it out."

Genius! I thought. Even something seemingly as insurmountable to outsiders had relevance in my world with OCD, and no one laughed at the question. We were all at different places in our personal relationship with OCD and on different parts of the spectrum, and all that was okay.

> ## How wonderful it is that nobody need wait a single moment before starting to improve the world.
>
> **—ANNE FRANK**

In another discussion, there was a beautiful blonde gal, and they presented her as the face of OCD. I thought OCD is so insidious that no one in a million years would even think this girl ever had a problem; on the outside she looked so put together. OCD has all sorts of hiding places.

My takeaway was that we were all being *robbed*! Robbed of precious time and robbed of precious life. I was quite done with mental bullies and vowed to do something about it! I wanted to be on the team with the helpers. I would do whatever I could to try to end some of the suffering with them. And that's when I got the first real flash of writing the book. I remember Dr. Daniel Kalb saying something like this to me: "It's great when sufferers can reach the point where they say, 'I'm willing to take the hit of anxiety, in order to free myself, so I can live in accord with what's really important in my life. I'm willing to put my energy into tolerating doubt and uncertainty, instead of squashing it, so I can move in the direction of my values.'"

The Egg Story

Several months later, I was in the grocery store for a quick in-and-out visit. I put what I needed into my shopping cart and headed to the register to check out. When I got there, a cashier was ringing up a lady's groceries. The cashier was a young man, and for his entertainment, he thought he would mess with the boy bagging the groceries at the end of the conveyor belt. He said in a chastising tone, "Remember . . . Jerry . . . the eggs go at the bottom of the bag and the heavy stuff on top."

It was apparent that the boy bagging her groceries had Down syndrome. Jerry then said with frustration in his tone, "No. No. No. The eggs go at the top!"

"Noooo, theeeey dooonn't. The eggggggggs goooo at the bottom. Don't you remember?"

Jerry's face was turning red with frustration. "Eggs go at the top!" The menacing cashier replied, "Okay, then, it will be your fault if they're broken."

The bagger stuck to what he knew and kept the eggs at the top of the other groceries in the big bag. The lady whose eggs were in discussion was busy finding her checkbook and appeared not to have heard the exchange. I was going to jump in and referee, because my natural inclination was to help out the bagger, but a voice inside my head said casually, *Don't get involved. They seem to have worked it out. You want to get out of here, don't you? Just go about your business.*

Once my own transaction was done, I got out of there and into the parking lot with my bags (with no eggs in them) and headed to my car. I was going to just scoot out and not deal with it. Then *BOOM!* A voice in my head said, *Oh no, Kirsten. This is not the Kirsten that God made you to be. This is not the God you report to.*

I knew it was the truth. Time to walk my talk. I quickly got my bags into my trunk and headed back inside. *Fuck, can't I just be one of those people who buries what they see and just get on with it? Can't I be one of those people?* But, of course, I knew the answer.

I figured my moment with the cashier had passed, so instead of confronting him directly, I sought out the manager. I found him out on the store floor and asked him to come walk with me to one of the aisles so we could speak privately. But Monkey just had to have his say: "The cashier or this store manager could be a serial killer, you know!"

By this time I knew he wasn't, but before Monkey tucked away, he said, "You can never be too sure." I waved him away.

I explained to the manager what I'd seen and how disgusting it was that one of his employees would treat another one that way. I told him that if this teasing and mental abuse were flying under the radar, he needed to know and do something about it. I could feel the relief that I'd gotten the words out and where they belonged.

The manager assured me that everyone there loved Jerry, and that he in no way would let this behavior continue. He seemed very surprised that it was going on at all. He thanked me for coming to speak with him and said that Jerry would most definitely no longer be teased.

The manager seemed very sincere, and I was thankful. It felt really good to be a peaceful warrior. I thought on my way out, *Another mental bully down!* I was starting to really like that feeling.

Digging Deeper:
It Starts with a Dream

What if I could do something that could help other people? Sign me up!

Contrary to popular advertising, I am my *most unhappy* when I am navel-gazing. Jeez Louise, how I wish I could go back and tell my high school self this! I was tired of just being trapped in myself and so obsessed about what I did or didn't do. I saw the book that I could create in my imagination. Doug said that I had been writing this book for years and years and that I had just become more conscious of it.

My mission and drive were to do something good for other people: turn my personal story and years of pain, abuse, and learning into something beneficial for others. Helping OCD sufferers and those loved ones who are trying to understand them was my burning motivation. Oh, we were well past the spark. We were at bonfire!

Just like dancing with coworkers or practicing Monkey Kung Fu or packing for Vegas or sending a package in the mail, I have to start with, **"Let's do this!"** Being open to the idea was the first step.

It all started by laying down the first word. Like all first steps, it was scary as hell. I cried. Doug said, "This is a happy moment. You are finally writing your book." I said, "I'm crying because I know all the work ahead of me!" But with my imagination fully engaged and access to my brain juice, I believed that I could tackle the mercurial beast OCD and turn what potentially could have just been a shit pile of an OCD-infested life into something positive for other people who are suffering.

There are days when I am in the flow with my writing and giant tapestry weaving. There are other days when I try to find the right words and they disappear like schoolchildren running away from one another. My motivation and dedication were *you*. You can read that line again if you'd like. You kept me going. I was also *totally stoked* to think that I could turn all my wasted years into something beneficial for somebody else. Now that's the God I report to! I was fully on board.

Origami

In our next meeting Pam didn't say, "How is your OCD?" Instead, she said, "How is Kirsten?" She has such a natural way of getting right in there. It's as though she laid out a big picnic blanket under an oak tree and said, "Sit a spell; take a load off." So it was in this accepting, nonjudgmental, and peaceful space with her that I started to drop into even deeper waters with myself.

I told her that I had been doing some soul searching. I felt that deep down things that I don't really talk about, except to Doug, had made an impression on me. Like I was a fossil with historical information imprinted into me. Somehow I knew that I was still coveting and not experiencing deep peace, that there was still a crimp in the spirit hose.

Often over the years Doug had asked things like, "Why didn't you turn your dad in or tell your mom about everything that was happening when you were a kid?" I told him that I thought my mom knew all about my dad and his strangeness and that she must have been okay with it. I'd figured there was nothing I could do.

My mom's dad died when she was three, and Kent and Brian lost their dad to suicide. She saw the damage of what not having a dad could do. This was her frame of reference. My mom always thought that having a dad was better than not having a dad at all.

> Yes, it is better to look from the window than not to look at all, but to look through the window cannot be compared to the windowless sky.
>
> —BHAGWAN SHREE RAJNEESH

Mostly, I didn't even want to talk about it, so I buried it deep inside myself. But now I felt ready. Ready to take a look at the ugliness for what it was. I was willing to investigate and take stock of the things deep in my being that were dark and sensitive like cavities.

After opening the door with Pam, I started to talk more with Doug about my experiences with my dad, my soul fossils. I told him about a field trip we took in first grade. We were taking a bus to the zoo. My dad wanted to come with the class. This would count as one of his weekly visits. He brought a big bag of purple grapes and shared them with my other young classmates and me on the bus. Things seemed to be going well with him, and his visiting time with all of us seemed nice and pretty normal.

Somehow, though, when we got to the zoo, my dad and I were the last ones off the bus. We were considerably far back from the class. As we were walking toward the zoo, my dad put his hand down the back of my pants and cupped my bare bottom. I immediately was uncomfortable and ashamed and said, "Daddy, stop doing that!"

He didn't stop. So I grabbed behind me and tried pushing him away from me. He laughed and said, "What? Are you embarrassed? You shouldn't be embarrassed by your father. Are you embarrassed by your own bottom?"

I remember he chastised me further and I felt deeply humiliated. I did, however, get his hand out of my pants! This stuff messed with my head so much. I was supposed to love and trust this guy, and he just confused and terrified me. I always felt apprehensive around him.

I told Doug other stories about my dad, like the time he put new-born kittens into a clear baggie and tied the bag at the top with a twist tie. I remember hearing them mew and seeing their squinty pink eyes up against the plastic. He placed them in the water and sent them down the Fox River, literally. He told me that they would have a better life this way. I also told Doug about my father making me watch him expose his girlfriend's breast and nipple to me. He rubbed it so it would get hard; he said that he was teaching me what it was going to be like to be a woman one day.

I told him about how I used to help my dad clean pounds of his marijuana when I was only five years old. I remember picking out the stems and seeds. When I was in the fourth grade, I inhaled laughing gas with him and his friend one evening. His friend, whom I never saw again, had something to do with race cars and had a tank of nitrous oxide that we puffed from all night long. There was also the confusing time when he invited me to watch him masturbate his cat, Shanti, with a Q-tip when she was in heat. Later, when I was an adult, my mom mentioned to me that my dad was very touchy and curious about my vagina while he changed my diaper. She said that she found his fixation odd. I found out later that all these infractions were renting valuable space in my soul. Like in *Star Wars*, there was a disturbance in the force. I was unsettled, very.

Because my dad had partial custody of me, I went to his house every other weekend and spent three weeks with him in the summer from the time I was three years old until I got into high school. I don't have a single memory of a time my dad was *not* high on pot or other drugs, or scoring drugs from a dealer, or being a dealer himself, or sleeping off the side effects of a narcotics binge. It's as though he scrambled my innards from my heart to my mind to my soul. There was so much scribble there, and I just wanted straight lines. I always wanted straight lines. I could finally see why OCD had felt so welcome: It gave me something to cling to in all the stress. It had given my life order and me a sense of control, especially in my dad's presence.

In my adult life, in my thirties, I read an incredibly informative book called *The Sociopath Next Door* by Martha Stout, and it really cleared up a lot of my confusion about my dad and his ability to do the unconscionable things he did, with no guilt.

I remember reading something once about how life is like a theater and there are some people in your life who need to be loved from a distance. When you're a kid, that's not so easy to do. My dad was in my front row.

The confusing thing about my dad—and about loads of perpetrators of abuse—was that he was not all 100 percent bad. By all rights, I could have stopped loving him entirely, but I never did. I knew at a very young age that he was very ill, and for the most part I kept what he did to myself. I thought that exposing his secrets would make me a bad daughter. I didn't want to be a bad daughter to him.

Of course, I could write a whole book about my dad and my experiences with him, especially during the 1970s when I spent all those weekends and summer weeks with him. But he has stolen too much life already, not to mention the lives of other people whom I love dearly, and I don't want him to take over this book. But one thing is very clear and needs to be said: he is the one who made being emotionally available unsafe. I spent thousands of hours of my life trying not to be available, and OCD was so good at keeping me incredibly distracted. It was my survival. And now I had to go back and fetch myself.

Pale Purple Hue

My dad passed away in 2009. Doug, my younger sister Nicole (who had a different mom than me), and I saw my dad's dead body before his cremation. It was in a formal funeral home, in one of the north suburbs of Chicago. Several ceremonies were going on at once, it seemed, like this dead person in Salon A and this dead person in Salon B.

My dad, however, was not in a salon; he was in something more like a utility room that people didn't go into unless they were the funeral home's staff. My dad was not into pomp and circumstance. He would have been just fine with the casual utility closet good-bye; he actually would have preferred it. He would have said that it was more real than being made up and smelling like powder.

There he was on his back, lying on a hospital gurney-like wheeled cart. He was in the clothes he died in, a T-shirt and pants, and his skin was cast in a pale purple hue. There he was, and this was the end of the road, at least for this lifetime. In a big way, it was a relief, a relief that he couldn't hurt himself or the rest of us anymore. But it was now time for an earnest good-bye.

I arranged his T-shirt so he looked a little neater in his deadness. Somehow, I brought forth the spark of love for him that had always been there—although sometimes more tucked away than other times. My little sister hugged his somewhat bloated belly, and then she laid her head on his chest. "Love you, Dad." I said it, too. "Love you, Dad." OCD wasn't there with me. I was really there with no buffer whatsoever. What a powerful feeling, you have no idea. It was like being in a courtroom when the judge takes the gavel, hits the stand, and says, "All charges have been dropped and you are free to leave." I didn't want to be the jail keeper and secretly harbor any anger, resentment, and buried Frank pain any longer. I was letting a thousand balloons of pain go. Off you go now. Bye-bye.

I let go of the man that I always wished he would be, and I let go of the man that he was.

Before we left, I cut a few pieces of his white wavy hair for sentimental keepsakes for my sister and me. Later I tied a piece of gold ribbon around my white lock. It is in a soft burgundy pouch that I have tucked away in my purse. The great thing is, I don't check it and recheck it compulsively throughout the day to see that it is still there. I just believe that it is.

I wrote and read my dad's eulogy. I have sure come to know in my lifetime that people are multifaceted. I spoke only of his good qualities, the most radiant facets of his personality, like how much his sociology students enjoyed him and how he was very bright and charismatic with a strong wit, that he was entertaining to watch, especially when he played "Rag Mop" on the piano and did his best impersonation of Red Skelton.

Good-bye, Dad.

One Hot Plate of Custom-Made OCD Coming Right Up

OCD comes to people in different ways, and it shows up on the doorstep at different times. I have a friend with OCD who grew up in a very religious household. Her OCD manifested in having serious and debilitating morality issues, scrupulosity issues, and issues with being good enough to be accepted by God or whether she'd be sent to the devil because she wasn't truly good enough. From her experiences with organized religion and her parent's values, her OCD had a wealth of knowledge—just like she did. Her OCD took that knowledge and used it against her. Her custom-made OCD worked on her.

My friend shared with me that she felt guilty sometimes about having OCD. She said her childhood was good and normal and that she had great God-fearing parents and a solid family structure. She said nothing bad ever happened that she can pinpoint. She also said that she didn't have any trauma or really bad times to speak of. This brought her frustration; she saw how someone who was traumatized could "get" OCD but couldn't see why she would and felt guilty about it.

I know another guy who has no idea at all where his OCD came from. According to him, he did well until his second year in college. He sincerely could not think of one trigger that could have even started it. There was no big breakup with any girl, no real problems to speak of. He thought he was pretty normal overall.

It's all just baffling to him how his OCD, like a ninja, just appeared out of nowhere. He developed an eating disorder; he was very obese when I met him. He told me that at his workplace he got teased because he had to wear gloves all the time, even when typing. He said he got pretty good at it. He also shared that he had a trail of clothes on his floor in his apartment that had to stay there no matter what and that not one clothing item could be moved. He built trail after trail and clothes weaved all over his floor.

There are little girls that can't stop washing their hands, even though the skin on their hands is cracked and bleeding.

I have read stories of OCD sufferers terrified and unwilling to leave their parent's basements at any cost. They are fully enveloped by their own fear. I have a friend that shared this with me: His sister, who's lived in their parent's basement all of her young and adult life, had to come out of the basement one time due to a life threatening medical emergency. She insisted that she could only leave carried out by the paramedics on a stretcher, with her body perfectly stiff the whole way, wearing dark goggles and headphones.

OCD isn't just getting in the way; it is robbing lives. It is actively crushing souls of desperate, good, loving people, making them comply to all of its sick and sociopathic demands and under all, even the most bizarre circumstances.

I also read an OCD memoir about someone whose father was a staunch perfectionist and quite hard on him for as long as he could remember. This person developed the need to be perfect in everything that he did. To be an overachiever would be to put it mildly. These were the bars of his cage that confined him and prevented him from experiencing real joy and a restful state.

I also know of a man obsessed with blowing leaves off his driveway, off his grassy yard, and off his porch. He has been known to blow leaves with his leaf blower for four to five hours straight. I imagine that to him each leaf may seem like an imperfect ghost that he needs to erase, and I am sure he knows and believes all the reasons. He even goes out in heavy rainstorms and blows leaves *that to anyone else* don't even look like they are there.

When I started to put this book together, my ongoing motivation was to bring you something of real value that you could use as a tool to help you out of your unique gilded OCD cage, whatever shape it has taken. I wanted to offer insights from my personal OCD journey from helplessness to hopefulness, from mental illness to mental stillness. In the process of getting real with myself and with you, I had to become a deep-sea diver and discover some of the most uncomfortable parts of myself. It is my hope that by sharing, you get to your joy much faster than I got to mine. *Life is too short for blowing leaves for hours or whatever manifestation your OCD is wearing!* My observation is that we OCDers seem to get carried away in our own OCD trance; different things seem to compel different people. Again, making the mercurial nature of this condition a slippery one. We do such crazy things in an effort to somehow make things better (OCD logic, I tell you; OCD math do X and get Y).

What do you get carried away with? What is interfering with your really connecting with people, perhaps loved ones, experiences, and joy itself? There's a whole world out there beyond the compulsive leaf blowing, and we all can fill in our own blanks from there.

We all have our own stories of just how we got where we are, about the nurture we received and the nature that we came in with. And my story is not bigger or smaller than yours; it's just different. I am diving deep, and you are welcome to jump on my back and see what we discover together.

The Final Threat

The desire to be heard, known, and felt deeply never disappears.

—ROBIN STERN, PHD, AND DIANE DIVECHA, PHD, "THE EMPATHY TRAP," *PSYCHOLOGY TODAY*

I thought about Monkey and how he had the authority because he had the power. I was held captive. He was the epicenter of punishment and reward. He had my full attention. He was dominant and I was submissive for more years than I care to remember. He had the threats that he held over me, and he knew exactly what to do for me to become and remain his faithful puppet. He motivated me with fear, and I bought his whole rap. If I didn't do my drills right and perform just so, I believed whole-heartedly that terrible things would happen. For example, I might lose loved ones or have them killed in a heinous way. I might be murdered. Our houses might burn down out of my negligence. I might not be forgiven and be burdened with guilt into eternity. I might cause a horrible accident. I might lose all my friends because I was so disgusting. Someone in my family might go to prison even though they were innocent. And the list of threats goes on. My Chi wasn't in sync with the rest of me. I could fill a library with all the crazy things that I did just to get to a "right" moment and move forward.

I sort of sank into myself and felt a deep pause of reflection. Beyond all those things, those threats, those OCD motivators, there was the final threat.

To me, the final threat that Monkey held over me was buried so deep that I could barely see it. It's the place where I was the most terrified. I believed that Monkey could take me "there." I thought, *Where is this mythical place, or does it actually exist?* Then the last part of the origami paper unfolded, and I saw it before me.

That place was back at my dad's house, and I was in that bedroom. I remember the instability I felt when my dad would tuck me into bed. I would look into my dad's stoned pink-pinwheel eyes as he said he loved me before he went back to his party. He and his long-haired hippie friends were on the floor tripping on LSD and trying to lose their minds. "Dark Side of the Moon" was blaring, Chianti bottles used as candle holders were thick with dripping wax, and thick smoke bellowed from the weed being passed around. Just a warped wooden door between me and the insanity of the other side.

While trying to lie in bed, I felt so stressed, anxious, and completely unloved. A real fucking hotbed of anxiety. It was so painfully apparent to me at such a young age that deep down in my soul, as I laid there all alone, I had no safe place to land. This all imprinted deep inside of me, and Monkey used it—Monkey has used it against me for years. He held the final threat, of taking me back *there*, and I did such crazy shit so I wouldn't have to go back to that pain. I felt like I was seeing the petri dish of where I became most spiritually, mentally, and emotionally crippled. Where I would cry for hours until I exhausted myself and eventually drifted off. I would slip into my own psychiatric rabbit hole and into sleep. Was this soul fossil the breeding ground for my OCD?

I once read that free-floating anxiety is the most intolerable sensation a human being can experience, and that OCD might, in fact, be a defense mechanism of sorts designed to confront it. The theory goes that OCs "assign" their biochemical anxiety to particular fears (obsessions) so that they can then take ritualistic actions (compulsions) to feel as if they're at least doing something constructive.

—JEFF BELL, *REWIND, REPLAY, REPEAT*

I can see how Monkey had all the ingredients he needed to work on me! He had an arsenal of madmen (thanks, Dad) and instability to pull from to build my teetering base. I don't blame anybody for anything. I don't even blame Monkey. It was just my antidote to madness and instability that at the same time served to defeat me and hold me trapped.

I didn't want a place that Monkey could threaten to take me to any longer.

I feel love and compassion for my little self under that cold, worn, thin sheet in that dark bedroom! I AM Kirsten Weirdsten! That's me and I'll take her, all of her. I don't want her "there" anymore.

Does your OCD have a "final threat"—the place that you fear most and will do anything to avoid?

Yes

I was feeling more and more soul space being relinquished, and it was the perfect complement to having more brain juice. I wanted to exchange all the pain for something else, and I just desired so greatly to move on. I was so tired of chasing ghosts and being afraid of life and all its uncertainty and messiness. I was tired of dodging my buried, painful soul fossils and finding a million distractions to not have to deal with them.

I had been running from myself and for so damn long.

I wanted to take part in another story, and I wanted things other than my pain to define me. I wanted to grab the pen and become the writer of my play.

Above all, be the heroine of your life, not the victim.

—NORA EPHRON IN AN ADDRESS TO THE GRADUATES OF WELLESLEY IN 1996

Just as I said yes to dealing with the anxiety instead of doing my compulsions, I say yes to my whole ugly mess. There is so much ugly shit, and I am just so over it. I said yes to all my imperfections. I said yes to not having everything be el supremo all the time like my OCD wanted it to be. Yes to life and its scariness. Yes to never living in a Mr. Clean commercial (although they do make everything look so good and appealing, it's fucking compelling). Yes to being flawed. Yes to OCD. Yes to being human. Yes to my own fractures. Yes to my own pain (the pain I have caused and the pain I have endured), and yes to every trespass before and behind me. I stopped holding anything hostage. I forgave myself, and that opened the door to me forgiving others. I didn't want to run anymore. I said, "Yes," and in a way, I surrendered. It's kind of backward, but what I have found is that there is power in surrender.

As time went on, I began to understand and forgive myself a bit better and all of my bad choices, one after another after another. Rather than working awfully hard to keep it all pushed down and present a "normal" front, I began to accept it all as *my story* and *my bullshit*. I didn't just want the life of a puller, taking in too much and feeling toxic by it all and just rolling from one suffering moment to the next. I didn't want to be the spiritual city dump any longer. Sure, I wish to God that my circumstances had been different, that I could have had spiritual guidance and stability, and not have felt so terribly alone, but they weren't there. There is peace alone in accepting my own mess and just how I got here, and there is peace in forgiving others, and, yes, there is even peace in forgiving Monkey.

It's been 14 years since John died. I still miss him every day, but I have learned to cultivate joy and peace in every breath, even though I feel that pain. You have to do them both at the same time. It's like a garden: you have to take care of the weeds, but you also have to plant flowers. If you only weed, you'll be exhausted and lose hope. And if you plant enough flowers, eventually there will be less room for all the weeds.

—SISTER D, "ZEN LESSONS ON HEALING AFTER LOSS," *PREVENTION MAGAZINE*

I even came to love Monkey in a strange way. If Monkey was like a sour stomach, love, I found, was like baking soda: it can take away the acid and the burn. **LOVE.** I know this seems radical! Why love an enemy, why love your OCD? Shouldn't you just hate it? This is what I have come to learn:

LOVE—it's here that you will dance out of your constriction.

It's available to you, too, and you can start from where you are right now. That's the most amazing part of all. You don't have to wait for anything. You don't have to wait for the right moment or the next compulsion being served. It is right now.

Tara Brach talks about turning arrows into flowers, and I get it! Love both toward myself and my OCD. You can't buy it. But you can grow it! I am on my way to fifty years old while writing this book, and I just now get the math! Love for myself and for my Monkey is the key that offers the freedom and peace that I have been searching for.

Like Bernie, my spiritual traffic guard I met when I was in my twenties, said, "You've got to do the dance." Because the math goes like this: The larger your heart gets, the smaller their weapons get.

If you want to learn to love better, you should start with a friend that you hate.

—ANTHONY MISSICO, JR.,
POSITIVE THINKING

My love enveloped Monkey, this broken, mean, and misguided soul. Once I loved all of me, lumps, bumps, moles, warts, Monkey, and all (it is no easy task), something wonderful happened. **Monkey transformed!** He became less of Monkey and more like a **Chimpsay** and love kept growing and from the most unusual and unexpected place—from what I deemed a character flaw within myself. I remember, in playing the card game War with my brother Brian, that the ace always wins. In the game of life, in the game of OCD, love wins.

Let this moment of compassion for yourself through. I see the beauty in you. I wrote this book because I love you. My love for you is a straight line from me to you, no scribble. I want you to have a big happy life. YOU DESERVE IT! Step aside OCD, step aside! Let the driver through! You!

Sometimes in life you have to get behind the wheel; then you learn how to drive. This seat is saved, and this seat is for YOU!

At first, you'll have to keep both hands on the wheel. But . . .

YOU'VE GOT THIS!

I started to see my Chimpsay as a somewhat cute prankster who was always up to something and trying to get my attention. But he was not to be feared. With Chimpsay, I came to a compromise. I figure that he will always be with me, so I might as well get along with him and love him, for that matter.

I was in a new groove with OCD.

MY LIFE WITH CHIMPSAY

Artist: Shawn Dickinson

himpsay says, "Hey, I have a problem for you. Don't you want to hear about it? I have a riddle for you. Don't you want to solve it? What if something catastrophic happens because you don't do your checks?!"

"Chimpsay, when you ask, I answer, '**Not today, Chimpsay! Not today!**'

"Next, Chimpsay, you're going to tell me that the house is going to burn down. **Yes, Chimpsay,** and I hope the flames are big enough to toast marshmallows! I love toasted marshmallows, Chimpsay!"

Vroom, vroom, and you keep driving toward what? Driving toward your big, happy life. See it in your mind's eye and head that way with intention, and believe in yourself.

Then Chimpsay pipes up again, and YOU AGREE.

YES, CHIMPSAY, EVERYONE IS GOING TO DIE A THOUSAND DEATHS.

EVERYTHING YOU SAY IS TRUE;

HOWEVER, I AM PRESSING ON!

I HAVE OTHER THINGS TO DO.

The most important thing to do at this time is to press on, no matter how uncomfortable you get. This way, you get bigger, and OCD gets smaller, and once again OCD is put into the side car. *Vroom, vroom.*

And remember this:

When I don't try to solve Chimpsay's riddle,

I put my mind at ease.

When I do try to solve the riddle,

I embrace insanity.

The more you can do this dance with your OCD, the better. The more you do it and the more you practice it, the sooner it will become automatic. Then Chimpsay's voice will eventually fade, and you will be able to tune in to other radio stations instead of just W.O.C.D. You and Chimpsay will be looking together in the same direction, right into the new bull's-eye, *into your well-being.*

For Chimpsay and me, this is not a dress rehearsal; this is life. And I am no longer waiting for my real one to start. This is living in the dash and not allowing OCD to rob me from any more precious time or keep me away from really being available to others. I would like to say that I am the driver 100 percent, but that wouldn't be true. When I stray, I just try to nudge myself back with loving kindness and awareness and get back into the driver's seat. Tara Brach mentions something like this in her teachings; the concept is about meditation and what you can do when your mind strays.

Dorsal Fin

The dorsal fin on a whale is an indicator of how the whale is feeling. I know of a story where, in captivity, one whale's dorsal fin was mostly down. It was just sort of limp and hanging listlessly to the side. However, once the whale was back in the ocean, taken out and away from captivity, his dorsal fin went back up and stayed up most of the time.

What I am going to share with you now is how I got my dorsal fin up. Perhaps you are an idealist and ask, "Is there a way to keep it up all the time?" I don't know about that, but I do know that when you are in balance—body, mind, and soul—it's harder to be thrown off, whether it be by a sociopath or whoever or whatever, including most certainly your OCD. I just don't make myself available to them.

At first, wellness became my revenge, and after incorporating it into my routine for years, it has become more my lifestyle. Doing exposure therapy whenever I get a chance to is also a part of my lifestyle and my intensive OCD self-management program. Life throws a lot at us humans, but we have to get back up off the floor if we want to really live and be a part of the dance of life.

Yoga

To be part of that dance, I thought that I would try yoga again. What did I find out?

It is so much more pleasant now that my OCD is in my intensive management program and now that more mind space is available (and spiritual space is freed up).

What I like about yoga is that I concentrate on breathing and stretching. I also get to concentrate on being present with soothing music that is relaxing. It definitely helps to keep Chimpsay and me in tune. My inner narrator also gets a chance to be calm and slow down in today's busy world. Yoga is about harmony and not about competition. I also really like the names for various positions, like the popular downward dog. Rocket does this move all the time. He is a very good stretcher and seems to know just when to do it.

I find yoga both freeing and invigorating. It's a chance to feel in the flow and align my chi. It's much different than experiencing OCD. Maybe yoga would be the same for you. But it's perfectly fine if it's not. The important thing here is finding something relaxing for yourself that doesn't cause you or others harm. For me, yoga is a time to get centered, recharged, and refreshed. When you can learn how to relax and practice doing it, if you're like me, you will be much less likely to immediately redline and have an OCD freak-out.

Where the Wave Meets the Sand

I decided to give meditation a shot. *Why not?* I thought. It just seemed to be part of my having-courage-to-deal-with-myself plan. I had heard and read that meditation can help you to silence your internal dialogue in order to find clarity and stillness. I thought it sounded relatively simple now that my OCD was so much better: clear your mind, sit, and settle in with yourself. I knew Chimpsay in my side car might make it all extra challenging, but I had no idea what I was in for.

Ancient Pali texts liken meditation to the process of taming a wild elephant.

(Jeez. Monkey chatter, having the heart of a lion, and now taming a wild elephant? Sounds like a flippin' circus! Where's the cotton candy? Someone bring in the clown!)

Here's my little song. It's a good reminder of why I try to stay present and mindful:

I TAKE A PAUSE AND DO MY DANCE,

BUT DON'T GET IN MY MONKEY TRANCE.

LIKE A DREAM STATE . . .

WHERE I DON'T SEE STRAIGHT . . .

I DON'T HAVE A CHANCE . . .

ONCE IN THE TRANCE . . .

AND THIS IS WHY I DO MY DANCE!

(I would just love to hear Eminem rap to my words! On the hierarchy of likeliness scale, it gets a low mark! I can dream, can't I?!)

I found a Zen Buddhist temple where a group practices meditation on Saturday mornings. It was sort of funny to me that I was trying to find sacred space within myself in a group setting. It was also funny that I drove in somewhat busy traffic to get to solitude. Life does offer irony!

I didn't know what to expect when I got there, but I assumed the environment would be very chill. When I arrived, my heart was pounding rapidly because I didn't leave myself enough time to get there (an old pastime that only jacked up my OCD tendencies further).

I sort of followed the people in front of me. They took their shoes off; I took my shoes off. They bowed to the lady standing shoeless on the carpet wearing what looked like a beige martial arts outfit; I bowed to the same lady. It's like we fully greeted one another. It seemed respectful and a much different feeling than the one I have had when visiting most service counters at some present-day big box stores. This lady actually seemed happy to see me.

Then I followed strangers into this big room. Up front there was a shrine of red flowers, a gong, and a Buddha. On the floor all over the room in neat rows were square mats, and each one had a roundish cushion on top of it to sit on.

I saw some people before they sat on their cushion sweeping their hands over it and readjusting it. They were not neurotically looking for imperfections like I sometimes do; they just seemed to be treating it kindly and making it the best cushion that it could be. The large room was filled with quiet people sitting on their cushions with their eyes closed. Apparently, they were "meditating," and it was now my job to do this and I wanted to do it very well.

At first when I sat on my cushion, it felt weird, sort of like a lump in my butt. I closed my eyes and tried to get into the meditation scene. I remembered reading in the past that with meditation I should be breathing in and out and following my breath, and I most definitely should stop darting my eyes around the room to see what was happening around me. I didn't want to look like such a novice.

The idea was that I was supposed to sit still and empty my mind. If a thought came into my head, I should see it as a train car and not get on and go for a ride. Let it pass by. This was very similar to my strategy with my OCD. Hello, OCD! and then let it fade.

As I sat there with my eyes closed, my mind was very chatty. I sort of called things out to myself and made little snarky judgments inside my head about the surroundings and the people around me.

Boy, this all-wood floor is creaky. Jeez, all wood; this floor had to be expensive to put in. God, dude who is somewhere to the left, I thought I was late; you should have been on time. Lady in the corner, your little cough is really annoying. Next time, try a cough drop. I would start to feel peaceful and then my mind would go again. *Are we going to Costco after this? It's only fifteen minutes away, and we need celery for the chicken salad.* Me to my mind: *Okay, thank you*, mind, *for that. You are a train car; now go away!* Bye-bye, celery. I imagined it on a train whizzing by sort of cartoon style.

Clearing my mind was challenging. Just sitting was challenging.

Sometimes I got fidgety and opened my eyes to peek at everyone meditating. I got a terrible itch on my leg. I remembered reading about this. The idea was that if an itch came, don't scratch at it; just acknowledge the itch and let it pass. I was not ready for that! I scratched and scratched and scratched (clearly a sign of a novice)!

I wasn't sure exactly how much time had passed, and I knew looking at my cell phone was not the right Zenful idea. Let me just say, it felt like a mighty long time. I did not get to the Promised Land, not even close. I just sort of babysat myself and my mind. However, just as I was starting to mellow and sink into it a bit, and put my mind down for a nap, finally, *GONGgggggggggggggggggggggggggggggggggggggggggggggg*. Out of what seemed to be nowhere, an older guy wearing, you guessed it, a martial arts outfit hit a gong up front at the shrine. The unexpected vibration from the gong reverberated down through my spine and out into me. It's as though it was breaking through any density that I had in me. It felt surprising, really good, and cleansing at the same time. The gong sound stayed in the room and in my body an incredibly long time.

The lady that I had bowed to on the way in was up front now, and she welcomed us to the temple and said that she was going to share a reading with us. She asked us to move in and sit closer to her. Her story was about a monk who was on a journey and could bring only a few things. "What did he really need with him?" she inquired. I think the monk opted for a bowl and some sort of knife. I saw the symbolism like this: When you boil it all down and simplify your life, what do you really need to survive? I thought a little bit about how we are all so complicated and have so much stuff (including all the stuff continually streaming through our minds, like celery for chicken salad!).

One lady, however, did not see the symbolism. She raised her hand, and when she spoke, she was very distressed. "How the hell am I supposed to pay my bills with a stupid bowl?!" I felt that this might be the last time I saw this gal here. After some more comments and questions, we did some chanting. Before we chanted, we were told the meaning of what we'd be chanting. It was about being a dedicated and loving person and being a part of a universal ripple effect of sorts. Probably forty people—the whole room—were chanting and making unusual sounds together. I could feel the warm unity in the room from the one combined sound we all made together. I felt more connected to these strangers than I have felt at some family parties at the castle.

We concluded with a little more meditation. On the way out, I saw that everyone respectfully bowed to Buddha before leaving the room.

There were cups of warm tea waiting for us in the greeting area. I drank mine slowly. I felt very different from when I first got there with my heart pounding from running late. Everyone was speaking with a kind and soft voice and so respectful of one another.

When I sipped my tea, I was with the tea, and I started to feel *mindfulness*. I was right there with my tea and nowhere else, and somehow I was safe. I thought, *Cool*. This is kind of like those people seeming to be really with their cushions without distractions. Before I left, I went to the bathroom. While I was in there, I noticed the shelving on the wall and the many flower vases on it. I thought to myself that flowers must really be a part of things here, and I liked and connected with that. Interestingly, they were all glass vases, so the stems in the water and the crowns at the top would be seen.

· 9 ·
HABITS OF HAPPINESS

Something Bigger Than Myself

I went back to the Zen Buddhist temple many times, and each time I was able to quiet Chimpsay and the rest of my circus-like mind a little more. With time and practice, once I settled in with myself, I'd visualize a wide-open beach with the waves coming in and going out, and I'd focus on my breath going in and going out. I could almost feel my feet and toes burrowing into the cool sand and hear the sound of the powerful ocean. I was being a part of something bigger than myself and bigger than my mind. What relief that offered!

I allowed myself to become like a sandcastle made of wet sand drips, pouring and flowing, whole, yet soft. This was a sacred place, where the wave meets the sand, and we all surrendered; Chimpsay, my mind, and the elephant. We were just being rather than tied up to our anxiety, thoughts, judgments, and emotions. This was a safe place to land, and a safe place to take flight. This was the pause!

**It has been said:
"Stillness is the language that God speaks,
and everything else is bad translation."
Stillness is really another word for space.**

—ECKHART TOLLE, *A NEW EARTH*

The idea of being as still as snow can seep into other areas of my life, your life. Stillness can become a welcome state of mind; interestingly, with stillness, things can get lit up inside you like the Fourth of July. (Irony, I know!)

Retro-a-go-go! Today

Doug eventually left his corporate job and accompanying steady paycheck and came to work with me at Retro-a-go-go! I'm incredibly fortunate; he's the most talented artist and product designer/developer that I have ever had the pleasure to work with and learn from. When he was a young boy, a little schoolgirl invited him to her birthday party, and she wrote this in the invitation: "Doug, I would like you to come to my birthday party because you are a good drawer." She was wise beyond her years.

Great news! We graduated and moved the business out of our basement. The Retro-a-go-go! Studio is located in a quaint historic town called Howell, Michigan. In the main part of the historic brick building, Doug and I design and create everything. Our team assembles, packs, and ships all over the world, as well as warehouses our inventory. Up front we run our retro-inspired gift shop and antique store. We've been told that the look and vibe of it all reminds people of the set on the hit show Mad Men.

One thing has remained the same. We tune into our imagination station everyday. We make what turns us on and what we feel passionately about. Luckily, we never seem to run out of ideas or new things to create and make. He might say, "Hey I've never seen this in the marketplace . . . wouldn't this be cool?" Then I might say, "Let's make it!" Both online and in our unique store you'll find everything that we love leaning to and inspired mostly between the 1920s and 1960s. From oversized 1960s Halloween masks for wall décor to Doug's original art of zombie mermaids and tikis on men's ties to my vintage valentine collection on mirror compacts and everything in between. When in need of a great gift for yourself or a friend, we are the ticket. However, we are not for the faint of heart or those who like things politically correct, and you will see our smart-ass humor sprinkled throughout. But for the cats that dig us, they go absolutely wild for the stuff, and that keeps us making even more—real embers in the fire.

Expanding beyond reproducing and repurposing Doug's and my personal art collection was the right thing to do for the business. Retro-a-go-go! is an official licensee of General Motors, Ford Motor Company, and famous 1950s pinup Bettie Page. We partner with these great brands and have access to their amazing art archives of vintage ads, emblems, and photographs, and in some way we feature them on all kinds of interesting, fun, and functional, pop-culture-themed products.

At the time of writing this book, Retro-a-go-go! has more than eight hundred products in the Retro-a-go-go! collection available to the end consumer and to stores. Our products have been in close to three thousand specialty boutiques and mid-tier chain stores across the world—all over the United States to the United Kingdom, Sweden, France, Spain, Japan, Switzerland, Canada, and many more.

In the twelve years Retro-a-go-go! has been up and running, we've met and shared time with many wonderful people who have become some of our best friends. Also, along the way we've had the opportunity to spend time in wonderful and amazing places. We exhibit and are a part of some terrific counterculture and pop-culture shows like Viva Las Vegas, San Diego Comic-Con, and even Monsterpalooza, where I unexpectedly got to meet Dick Van Dyke! Truly a great experience to look up from the booth and see him right in front of me.

Supple Noodle (Plus They Make for a Much Better Soup!)

There's an art to flexibility, and developing this stance doesn't come easy to those of us with OCD and high anxiety either. I work on it every day, no kidding.

What's my travel secret now? Sometimes I joke with myself by saying the perfume I wear when traveling is "Surrender." The perfume called "Resistance" is not nearly as delightful. Now I go into the process of traveling less dense and more flexible, like a cooked spaghetti noodle that is fluid instead of an uncooked one that can *crack in half* and *freak out* at any upset—of which there are potentially hundreds, change that, thousands. Being present makes me feel more secure about the moments and what I'm doing with more certainty. The airport, Vegas, and casinos may never change, but my reaction to them can. Just remember what Dr. Wayne W. Dyer in his book, *Everyday Wisdom*, said: "You can't always control what goes on outside, but you can control what goes on inside."

I used to avoid things that could ratchet up my stress, such as packing a suitcase, and waited until the last second to deal with them. I have learned that things go a lot better if I allow myself more time. That's not more time for cord checking or stove or door checking either. It's more reasonable time for myself to do the things that need to be done without adding unnecessary stress. Stress and OCD can be addictive; they're a real lightning bolt to the system. Now I prefer other ways to tap into my energy reserves.

Now when I leave for a trip, I say out loud, "This is going to be an adventure." This head-set works much better than fear. I accept that I will at times be uncomfortable, probably a lot, but I will get through what comes my way. Sometimes I even get excited about the adventure up ahead instead of plowing into my own worry and dread of *what could be ahead.*

My life has been full of terrible misfortunes, most of which never happened.

—MICHEL DE MONTAIGNE

Also, I don't have to be a perfect packer like I used to force myself to be. I do my best, and if I don't have something that I need when I get to my destination, I'll buy it there. "Oh lookie here, I thought I would be zigging (brushing my teeth right now) and instead I am zagging (running out to the store to buy a new toothbrush)." There's no need for the sky to fall. I just dust myself off and do what has to get done rather than allow OCD to drag me around like a rag doll.

This is a biggie for me: I allow myself one check as I leave for my road trip (determined by me! And why just one check? Because this seems like what a non-OCD person would do to ensure safety). This is where mindfulness really comes in nicely. I am fully present (and not in Monkey trance) for one door check, one wallet check, one stove check, one faucet and running water check, one ID check—you get the idea. Knowing that there is only one check allowed for me means I have to come to the table *as alert as fuck*.

Getting through airport security often consists of waiting in line and being in that mental idle mode. For me, this time can be challenging, and my OCD mind can pop up with a variety of questions: Did you leave the stove on? What if this show is not worth all the effort? What if this guy in front of you is a serial killer? What if on this trip you misplace your wallet? What if you are in line so long that you miss your flight? I say, "Thank you for your questions, but I am not interested."

If I do step onto the anxiety train, I try to say, "Oops, I see where I am; I need to get off this thing." I don't want to add to anyone's potentially shitty day with me being bent out of shape and not okay with myself. One thing I have found is that if I address the people that I interact with as friends, often they address me right back as a friend. All in all, there is less suffering for everybody. Really connecting with people, even perfect strangers, with a shared laugh or a knowing look is one way that I do this.

I do my best to try to read and react to what's ahead; there can be a certain pattern to it, and by now it is familiar. For instance, I know I will be taking off my shoes as I go through the security check, so I wear slip-ons (when I remember to). I have sensitive ears, and sometimes the forced air on the plane or in the terminal messes with me. Do I look perfect and *Vogue*-like sitting on a plane in June wearing black earmuffs? Of course not. I probably look like a loon to most. But like a good mom or dad packing lunch for their child going on a field trip, I prepare for myself. I become like my own caregiver and pack caringly and lovingly for myself, and yes, that includes healthy snacks! Do I find myself sometimes eating fatty fries when I should be eating cucumber slices? Sure. The idea is to implement an internal wellness compass and get back on the wellness path.

Do annoying things still happen? Yes. However, I am just a lot less annoyed. I try to cope with the data input differently.

For instance, it's easy to get stressed waiting for the lady to get her suitcase secured in the overhead compartment in front of me on the plane. My inner narrator could say, "God, Fucking Lady, why is this taking you so much fucking time?!" and ratchet my own stress levels. Or I could just replace "God, Fucking Lady" with "Kirsten, relax; you'll get to your seat when you get to your seat. No need to blow a gonad." Now I try to be that loose supple noodle, not the uncooked one. I have other options in the moment than losing my shit. Maybe I could ask if this lady needs my help. Or while she is busy doing her thing, I can look around for a kid with an *excited to be traveling smile* on his face or a senior citizen with a sparkle of wisdom in her eyes. I shift my attention to something I might find more pleasant than feeling incredibly stressed inside by this lady's action. Am I like a centered monk and have love only for the kid behind me violently kicking my chair? Oh, hell no. Believe me, other emotions do come to the surface; I am human, after all!

And I remember this from the book *Drinking: A Love Story* by Caroline Knapp, the acronym **HALT**. This reminds me to never get too **h**ungry, **a**ngry, **l**onely, or **t**ired (p. 242). These are known hotspots for alcoholics and OCDers alike.

Next up, two concepts I embrace: "Behind the Waterfall" and "In the Pocket." They're both such good ones, and I am looking forward to sharing them with you now.

Behind the Waterfall

Presence has two interdependent qualities of recognizing, or noticing what is happening, and allowing whatever is experienced without any judgment, resistance or grasping. Presence is our deepest nature, and the essence of meditation is to realize and inhabit this whole and lucid awareness.

—TARA BRACH, "HOW TO MEDITATE"

Can you take meditation with you, or does it stay behind on the round cushion at the temple? Applied Buddhism means that *mindfulness happens all day*. I find mindfulness to be wonderfully rewarding. It's nothing lofty or out of reach at all. It's like I can submerge more into my being, rather than focusing all over the place like a scattershot with the energy of a hummingbird and the vibe of a chainsaw.

In his book *10% Happier*, Dan Harris shares that a good place to be is behind the waterfall. It's *a meditative pose.*

Tumbling down through the waterfall in front of us are all the things going on and passing by throughout our day, throughout our moments, whether you are at the airport or somewhere else. The idea is that you try not to attach to any of the ever-changing stimuli before you. You're not mentally gripping on to all or any of it.

If I find that my inner narrator is having a full boardroom discussion in my head, I do what I can to bring myself back to being present.

I have heard that stress is when you are doing something you don't think you should be doing. So, for instance, when I am in traffic, sure I wish I wasn't, but I try not to have a conniption fit and lessen my life span and start pumping cortisol into my belly. I accept it and sit with it no matter how unpleasant it may seem. If I have a tizzy and say, "I should be at home cooking! Damn this fucking traffic!" *Bah bam!* Hello, Stress! It's sort of accepting what is rather than becoming derailed by what isn't.

So what about this? If your OCD has a gift for you, say no thank you to the gift. If your version of Monkey has a riddle for you, say no thank you to the riddle. If Monkey has a problem for you, say no thank you to the problem. If Monkey has something that he wants to show you, say no thank you to what he wants to show you. If Monkey has a challenge or a game for you, say no thank you to the challenge and the game. Learn to notice without being trapped.

In the Pocket

I once heard a musician talk about being "in the pocket" when playing an instrument. He said it was like slipping into a pleasurable space, like a welcoming groove inside himself, and he gives himself to it. When I write, sometimes I'm "in the pocket," and those are some of the best times. It's sort of like I do a submarine thing and sink into myself a little bit (thank you, meditation practice).

Park Amidst the Palms

Our biggest Retro-a-go-go! show of the year is in, you guessed it, Vegas! Another big buffet plate full of Vegas! It's the ongoing theme that seems to come with running this business. Exposure therapy central! It's easy to get swept away in all the energy and begin to feel overwhelming stress.

The show we do is Viva Las Vegas, and our work hours are taxing, and the show goes on for days on end. Frequently, as I need to truck through the casino, when I start to feel too off-course and hurried, I remind my inner self to "park amidst the palms" *in my mind and in my being.*

Sometimes I have to switch it up; I don't always want to be behind a waterfall or in a pocket!

Okay, I cannot write a complete book without including this next story.

I have a good friend named Bob. Since I am from the Midwest, he says that I say his name "Baab." He and his wife sell vintage clothing at the Vegas event every year, and it is always a joy to see them, worth the trip alone.

Baab is diabetic and ran into some real trouble within the last year. A nail went through the bottom of his shoe and lodged into his foot. He did not know it was there festering and the wound becoming infected because his feet were numb from not taking care and being a better manager of his diabetes. Long story short, Baab had to get his right leg amputated below his kneecap. He spent the entire time at one Viva Las Vegas event getting around by wheelie cart with his amputated leg on a flat board and his left leg doing all the work of pushing and keeping him moving. He has become very knowledgeable about his diabetes, and he is now dedicating himself to being as healthy as he can be. However, he is not beating himself up about the loss of his leg, and he is not weeping in a heap with tremendous resistance. He is starting from exactly where he is.

Baab and I were able to catch a break and spend a little time together running errands, buying rubber bands for holding Doug's rolled-up art prints, highlighters, and more candy for the booth. He said, "You know, Kirsten, what having my leg amputated is really all about? **Adapting**." We just sat there and sort of absorbed that powerful word. I felt like I was absorbing real wisdom.

Sure, he'd rather zig, have his leg, who wouldn't?! But he's going to zag and figure out the best way to deal with what he has. It's not resistance. It's acceptance. Once his amputated leg atrophies, he will get a prosthetic one. He's looking forward to seeing what is available and to picking one out. He makes it sound super fun, like picking out a skateboard or something.

Traveling to India

For business, I traveled to San Diego Comic-Con. As usual, the crowd was bananas! I was exhibiting my biz and had a booth by Funko and Marvel Comics. It's moments like these when I think, *Hmmm . . . maybe I've made it.*

On move-in day, the truck with all our products and displays was late, so I had unexpected time on my hands. Old Kirsten would have gotten all tight and freaked out about being off schedule. New Kirsten said, "Well, I will make the best of it." I found a gem of a spot nearby and discovered a strip mall with all Indian Hindi stores. They had everything—from fruits I had never seen before to amazing colorful fabrics and interesting groceries to the blackest eyeliner I have ever seen. I was in the moment and not swept up in anxiety. After all, I got to see some new things! Sometimes the unexpected can be joyful if we let it be. Rather than making me mad or frightened, I was refreshed and recharged by the unexpected. The truck did eventually arrive with all our display fixtures, products, and everything we needed to exhibit at this Con, but first I got to go on a little trip to India.

Unlikely Hero

Another time I was in the middle of a trade show where we were exhibiting (you guessed it, in Vegas! Again!), and I was doing my job as the company's spokesperson, interacting with customers and sharing or introducing our new products to them or fluffing up the booth.

I received an unexpected phone call, and I was told that my mom's husband, Richard, was near his death. He was in the hospital with all kinds of things going wrong and rapidly. When I understood the severity of his condition, I immediately flew home. A responsible and relatively new Retro-a-go-go! employee took the lead from there and handled everything so I could go be with my mom's husband probably for the last time.

All of our time together, Richard's and mine, over the decades wasn't wonderful; however, I wanted to be there with him before he passed *as much as our relationship would allow.* In his nearly silent hospital room, where he lay on his back underneath a thin blanket, we all took turns sitting on the chair next to him and being with him. It was now my time to be with Richard. Other people were in the room sort of watching and hanging out but trying to be quiet.

I held Richard's hand while I was weeping, and I told him in my crackling voice how thankful I was that he was a good friend to my mom over all the years and that I loved him.

He was too weak to say any words or open his eyes, but he raised his eyebrows up and down to let me know that he was hearing me. This was our final dance.

I heard later through one of his six sons, I don't remember which one, that right before his death, his overseeing nurse privately said to him and his son that the only way he could stay alive any longer was to start being fed through a tube directly into his stomach. He was a stubborn one, even until the last minutes of his life. There would be no feeding tube.

Lying there, weak as hell and almost unable to speak, his last words were, "Let's do this!" And he marched alone right into the very face of his own death; I will forever be in awe of his courage. **"Let's do this!"** really sticks with me and makes me smile a little thinking of his tenacity. It's like death was the big old dog in the room facing him, and Richard said, "Come here, boy."

Mosaic

Here's one way to look at life and OCD together: imagine standing in a tide pool next to the ocean. The water is cold and crystal clear. You look down at your feet and see stones, pebbles, sea glass, and little shells in various shapes and sizes. Some stones are orange and rust-colored with beige swirls, some stones are black and slick like smooth whale skin, and there's bluish-green sea glass and soft golden sand. We all get to see something different when we look down. It's our pattern; it is our life and everything in it from our own perception.

Sometimes we want to capture and control the pattern we see and not allow for change. With OCD, we do our compulsions in an attempt to arrange and glue stones down like glued tiles in a mosaic. However, like life, the ocean has a strong current and is forever changing. Our stones, pebbles, shells, and sea glass will tumble and toss, in and out, no matter how hard we try to lock them in place. It's life, and shit is going down, and stories are unfolding for all of us. Stories of life, stories of death, of rebirth and destruction. Things are constantly flowing and changing; this is the very nature of life. These things are inevitable for all of us.

OCD operates differently than the nature of life. OCD trains you to not let go, to clamp down like a mo fo, and to fear the next wave of change and to fear feelings of not being in control. However, there is only letting go and being ready for the next pattern to come. Intellectually, I know this; however, being accepting of it is not necessarily easy.

My mom, for instance is like a beautiful transparent pink piece of sea glass; in one way or another, she has always been in the pattern I see, in my life as I have always known it. I love her in every way imaginable and try to soak up every second when we are together. One day, I will have to give her back to the universe; back to the ocean from which she came (eventually we have to give everything back). The sea glass that means so much to me may tumble away; however, my deep love for her and all of our experiences here on this earthly plane are the *treasured soul fossils. Here's the great news: Those you get to keep!*

I cannot do anything to interrupt the flow of life, no matter how hard I try to freeze time and try to make scary and sad moments not ever come again; they're coming. Like it or not, my own death is coming, so I better start living but certainly not live under the heavy hand of OCD. I just have a short window while I am here, everyone does, and the best that I can do is live and love with intention and really go for it!

Where I Am Today

Sometimes I write on a sticky note and toss it onto a stack of mangoes. . . .

Let me just say, exposure therapy is ongoing, and there are opportunities to do it everywhere. With purpose, and an available mind, I take opportunities to not go the way my OCD wants me to go. I no longer straighten soup cans on the shelf so they all face forward. When I pick out plums, they don't need to be perfect. Actually, I challenge myself not to get only the 100-percent-perfect ones but to get some medium-perfect ones, too. Buying all bruised, though? Now that's throwing money away! So I work within a range. I try to gauge what would be the normal range for a non-OCD person.

Remember that OCD is specific. It gives you no margin for error, no margin for "a range" with anything. It's black and white. I find that having a range, allowing some gray, is so much easier and so much more enjoyable than having a specific target, even with my weight. I have a healthy range for myself instead of a specific number. What would a healthy person do? In my mind's eye, I try to imagine my most healthy self and behave like that person as much as I can. When I get off-track, I try to nudge myself back with loving kindness instead of beating myself up with an invisible club like I did for years in the past à la Sergeant, à la Monkey, à la Inner Narrator, à la Joy Killers.

What I believe about the future determines how I live now. I believe in a hopeful and promising future and try to tilt my sail that way. Is it easy all the time? Oh, hell no. But I am committed to where I want to go and committed to not going back to where I have been. I am in my own management program, my own healing program, and I always will be. I'll continue to tweak it as I go along. I have made it to this moment with you, and there are so many more places to go.

I want to be present for when the good things happen and not just swept away with my clobbering OCD mind. I want that for you, too.

Things are really good now, and that's a lot better than how they used to be. I have tossed cigarettes, street drugs, and drinking out of my lifestyle and that has brought more peace.

I have resigned from being General Manager of the Universe. That burden has been lifted off of my shoulders and it feels good! Maybe you'd like to step down from this position, too. This long awaited resignation was my big ticket out of having to control every little thing.

I need to remember that with OCD, there is no resolution to the riddles! I need to keep dealing with being uncomfortable when discomfort arises. Sometimes you have to break through being uncomfortable to get to comfortable. Retro-a-go-go! is still an excellent source of my ongoing exposure therapy, sometimes a little bit too much to the extreme for my liking, however! I need to keep trying to let go of my OCD thoughts when they arise, if they do arise. Staying interested in life and staying engaged with things other than Monkey helps, and so does helping others.

Partnering with Chimpsay is so much better than feeling ongoing desperation and suffering with Monkey. It is no longer just at the Zen Buddhist temple or when I am sitting and meditating that I can reach where the wave meets the sand. *That beautiful opening in life* is available to you, too; you just have to look for it. Like Dan Millman says in his book, there are "no ordinary moments." The big win is in the moments of life and being available for them. The thing about Monkey, my OCD, was just that it made me so goddamn unavailable. Now I control my attention. I choose the radio dial, and it is not W.O.C.D; it is W.Y.C.D. (Yes Can Do). This station is available to you, too. The first step is to be willing to turn the channel.

In today's life I am doing things I never thought were possible . . . and yes, I can eat ice cream and have some fun like my mellow chiropractor encouraged me to do so long ago, when it seemed so terribly out of range. Can I be silent in my own mind so that I can actually listen deeply to someone else? Yes! Is being present and available in a kind and compassionate way to someone or something one of the best ways to show them that you love them? Yes! Believe it or not, I enjoy the realness of sobriety (I know—so much different from the past). I am not as scared to stand there, wherever I might be, and embrace it. Like you, I am filled with all sorts of emotions, and for sure, some life stuff is scarier to me than other life stuff. There is a difference between real fear and OCD fear, and I work on being a traffic guard of the two constantly. With each exposure that I can embrace, more confidence is added to my satchel that my friend, Monkey, can never take away. I earned it and it is mine entirely. I have also found that really being available to someone—letting them know that you see them and hear them—is a wonderful gift.

Distracting Messages

It's easy to get caught up looking at our cell phones, playing with our electronics, or staring at the TV so we don't have to be fully and consciously present. It can be similar to an OCD trance, I tell ya!

It's challenging not to get ratcheted up by all the millions of messages flying into us like mosquitoes on a mission to penetrate flesh. We are all sort of under the siege and fire by continuous messages. They're coming from everywhere.

Here's a "for instance." There I was having just a moment with myself while pumping gas at the gas station. On the pump, a mini-TV screen was yelling at me about something, something they wanted me to do. It's like they said, "Hey, there's going to be a human being (a consumer zombie) standing here with eyeballs and ears. LET'S GET 'EM! FIRE!"

Like I have learned to do with Monkey, I said, "Not today, not today." At the pump I literally turned my head and looked away. I didn't appreciate that infringement on my being.

Chimpsay and His Messaging Center

Chimpsay is clever, no doubt about that, and I don't see that changing anytime soon. He may attract my attention and get me to start playing a game, but I do the best I can to catch myself and say, "Not today,

Chimpsay! Not today!" I continue to work away from mental illness and toward mental stillness. I find spending time with and in nature is a valuable part of my wellness. Such an antidote to our sped-up and demanding lives.

I have resolved to not live in a perfect world by OCD's rigid standards. Perception is key! Yep, lightbulbs will be dusty, I may not be able to ever wipe banana residue or pencil residue completely off my hands, I may forget to blow out a candle when leaving the house, and one day I may cause something catastrophic to happen. I accept these things and so many more so that I can really live fully and not in my OCD cage any longer. I'm participating in constant exposure therapy throughout each day as a practice that keeps me in tune and on track with my healthiest self.

Is It All Peaches and Cream?

AH, HELL NO. I am human, you know. I lean more into peace whenever I can and less into strife. Did I hit the roof when I got a $10,000 shipping bill that came in the mail at the Retro-a-go-go! Studio? **AH, HELL YES!** Do I cry sometimes after I hang up the phone with my younger sister, Nicole, and feel the distance between us? **AH, HELL YES!** Am I getting up in the middle of the night and binge eating? No! Am I allowing myself a healthy weight range instead of a finite number on the scale? Yes! Am I able to sit through an entire movie and get something out of it? Yes! Do I feel like my creativity is stuffed inside an acrylic box? No! Do I make spaghetti with meat sauce every March 12 for Rocket's birthday? Yes! Do I feed him at the table with a fork as he stands up on my lap? Yes! Do I like myself more? Yes! Do I love myself more and treat myself better and even with compassion? Yes! Are there exposure therapy opportunities everywhere? Yes. Am I happier now that I have given up being General Manager of the Universe? Yes! I have stepped down from that position, and more joy has entered my life. Is my dorsal fin more up than down? Yes! Is my state of being and how I see things a scribbly **kn**ot all the time, like it used to be? **Kno**!

Doing my compulsions perfectly isn't what matters anymore. Being available to my friends, family, and life experience is!

When I can, I like to spend some time at an animal shelter in a nearby town. I enjoy letting the cats out of their cages, giving them attention and love, and petting them if they want. I talk to each of them and ask them how they're doing. Their stories are oftentimes sad. I try to give them something other than more sad.

Without my OCD stealing the show, without the Ringmaster and the next hoop, I am so much more available to really be there with these animals if only for a little while, and as you know, I have some lost time to make up for! Being available is a gift to them and to me, too! Not to mention how fun it is. If they are scarred, I try to be a safe place for them to land. I hold their furry and soft cat bodies close to my chest and envelop them in love, and we park amidst the palms if only for a little while.

I like to bring the dogs to a nearby park. We walk a bit so they can stretch their legs. I like to play with them, toss a ball if they are interested, and always tell them that they're good doggies (they need to know this!). It is not pleasant bringing them back to their cages; often they pull and resist it. This is all the motivation I need to keep coming back!

Am I more of a pusher than a puller? I am both; it depends on the circumstance. I guess I finally and fully understand Dan Millman's book *Way of the Peaceful Warrior* that Bernie gave me so many years ago. When I can, I like to absorb the positive and show the negative the curb. This is an ongoing process; some days I am better at it than other days.

Maybe you'd like to write a letter similar to this—if not now, perhaps sometime.

Dear Sergeant from long ago, Addiction, Monkey, and Mind, and you, too, Chimpsay. Step right up, ladies and gentleman! Step right up!

And finish your letter with Caroline Knapp's quote from *Drinking: A Love Story*.

> *I will not take your spiritual carrot on a stick
> promising comfort and relief.
> I will sit with who I am.
> I will sink into myself without you. I am okay.*

Am I perfect? No. Will I falter here and there? Yes. I will make mistakes. I will fall down and get up again. I am a work in progress and I will be forever. But I know that there is always a new moment to jump into; we just have to see our way in.

While I was writing this book, of course, OCD things popped up. It is how I read them and react to them that make all the difference. It's taking that pause and recognizing it for what it is. The more I practice this, a cool thing happens: it all becomes much more instinctual and automatic, and it will for you, too.

Final Thoughts from Your Friend, Kirsten Weirdsten

These days, I go to sleep with Rocket's paw in my hand instead of cocaine crust in my nose. One of the things that I have learned along the way is that there is much joy in my still mind, and it is well worth developing. As part of my wellness quest, I have found that even five minutes of meditation, sitting still and quietly, can make a world of difference. I find it to be a way to readjust and refresh. Imagine a big book filled with loads of words, and you are reading, reading, reading, taking it all in until your eyes get tired. Then, voilà, you get to a page that is all white. Ah, white space; it's valuable. It's a place to land and give your eyes and mind a necessary break. When I can finally settle down with myself (which is tough sometimes), it's like finding some white space for my being, and, with continued practice, it seems more natural. Relaxing and being mindful are completely different than chewing on volts of anxiety. Mindfulness is worth developing; it's the skillful use of your attention to both inner and outer worlds.

Peace and mental stillness can be stronger than OCD, and that is exactly what OCD doesn't want you to hear. I love busting OCD! I have heard it said that submission can lead to rebellion, and I am living proof that this can be true.

I am avenging what I have lost, and I want the same for you.

In the past, first Sergeant and then Monkey grabbed a thought and said, "Let's freak out!" It could be random at times and very powerful. He picked the topic and pulled all the alarms. He was a big, overpowering mental bully who delivered the meals and said, "Feast on it!" There was a point that all I could do was follow Sergeant's commands and just try my best to prop myself up and keep going until I couldn't any longer and the china cups crashed.

My wish for you is that you can get off your journey of pain and mental bullying and jump the rail heading toward your big, happy life. Do your Kung Fu Dance Moves; stay limber on that dance floor. My OCD is much more manageable and my learning about it continues, but it will be a lifetime of learning. I have more imagination (brain juice) to access and time itself, and it was worth all the work to get here. Do I sometimes slip and find myself seemingly back at square one from time to time? Yes, but it is less frequent, and I am not nearly as terrorized or debilitated. Health of all kinds is the goal. I find that spiritual health is crucial to the mix as well as good nutrition and exercise. I try to read books and fill my mind with things and people "that up me at the fountain," like the man who upped me so long ago when I was a young girl needing a drink on a hot day at the beach.

I would also like to salute my mentor, Dr. Wayne W. Dyer. Sure, we never met in person; he passed away before I had the opportunity to actually meet him. However, he was a man "that upped me at the fountain." I thank God—I thank the universe—for connecting me to Dr.

Dyer through his writing, many books, and PBS presentations. He was truly the dad I never had! He opened my eyes to all kinds of possibilities and helped me tune up my spiritual compass. Life can be like sandpaper; it can be rough, throw us curveballs, and not seem fair, but it is in the way we interpret our life that becomes our reality. It is what we do with it that counts.

May Dr. Dyer forever rest in peace. But if I know him, he's busy right now in his dead business, doing some more cool shit and most definitely sliding down the rainbow and showing other angels how to do it!

It's difficult to have the right balance of all things in your life all the time. That kind of extreme thinking sounds very Sergeant and Monkey to me. People change, needs change, variables change. What I do recommend is *expanding your wellness campaign*, including loving yourself, warts and all. I found that accepting and loving all of me (which is not always easy: Hello, abundant arm chub that, no matter what, will not tone and overall body that wants to go the way of a beach ball) makes me feel more complete. I look to other well-being designers for helpful input. I have found so many great books and websites with applicable insights that I share in the "Further Resources" part of the book.

Now I work at replacing painful soul fossils with loving soul fossils. I also let good things make an imprint rather than sluffing them off and not giving them the same value as I once gave *my deep soul fossils of pain*. I allow myself to absorb the good stuff! I look for ways to give good stuff to others *but sometimes more successfully than other times*.

Dr. Hanson covers more stuff like that in his book, *Hardwiring Happiness*, and it's a great read. Look him up online; you can sign up for his newsletter, and he even knows about lighting up the neural circuits of happiness, love, and wisdom. This guy has it going on.

I gave my time to yahoos (of which there have been many), and now yahoos don't have a place at my table. Also, and I cannot stress this enough, having a good and solid partner who adds to the wellness path instead of taking it away means the world to your well-being. Make sure the people in your "front row" deserve to be there.

A big one for me is allowing only one check—no more—so I had best be fully present for my "one-check experience." As for cleaning the fridge, once every six months—I am guessing. It seems normal enough for me and, most importantly, not extreme (and not perfectly cleaned and scrubbed down either. Sure, there probably are pieces of old lettuce jammed up somewhere that I'm not getting to). I leave my sock drawers sort of unorganized on purpose! I let my hangers face all kinds of ways in my closet. I know, dare devil on the loose, right?!

Here are some good questions to ask yourself: Are you eating healthy, sleeping well, getting good physical exercise, being mentally challenged by something other than OCD, and finding ways to keep your brain stimulated but in a good way? Are you finding and doing positive things to keep your spirit alive? Are you doing things that play to and bring out your loving nature?

Lots to think about and manage, I know. I have found that balance and harmony are what to go for. Finding this balance does not need to be severe, however. I think finding a *healthy range* is what is important. I used to feel that everything had to be perfect, like a 100 percent++ on a school paper.

Now, if things are between 90 percent and 100 percent, damn, am I fortunate?! Ranges are tough for people with OCD, because OCD can be such a black-and-white universe. Accepting some gray has made me a lot happier. I have found that flexibility from my experience brings more joy than rigidity does (Go, supple noodle!). Remember, if you give a little room to your OCD it will take a mile, so in that case you have to be a strict manager! Keep an eye on him/her. I'm still very aware of what my OCD wants me to do, and I consciously don't do it. Not today! Not today!

Properly employed, the preceding tools can constitute quite an effective arsenal for managing your OCD, your mind, and your state of well-being. My resolution now is much different; I resolve that nothing is perfect. I resolve that exposure therapy keeps me healthy. I resolve that life is messy.

Remember, like me, you are the designer of you. You can find a wealth of books and information out there that can sharpen your awareness and get you in tune and informed about the things that I have been talking about.

Also, the way that you talk to yourself is very important, and how you conduct your inner monologues has an enormous effect on your success and how you feel on the inside. Your self-talk is a powerful instrument.

Socrates called this dialogue something like "the talk that the soul has with itself." If you are mindful and present, you can keep a close eye on your self-talk and redirect when needed.

I have also learned that you can have an epiphany anywhere; mine was looking at toilet seats, of all places.

Oh, and another biggie: at some point I will have to let go of this book and send it off to the printer. See, walking the walk, talking the talk.

During the process of writing this book and putting it all together, I have been in a world of scraps of paper. When I think of something to communicate with you, if my notebook is not handy I may write something down on a dinner napkin or anything I can get my hands on, fold it up, and put it in my purse or pocket for later review and reflection.

Doug recalls that when we lived in Benicia, California, we would spend hours upon hours talking about scraps of paper that I did, didn't, or might have written on and God forbid left somewhere. We talked about scraps of paper every day for hours on end. Poor Doug! (Oh, how I craved reassurance!) Thank God we are filling our time with more real and valuable things now!

The creation of the book is huge exposure therapy because it is writing on paper—A LOT OF PAPER—and releasing it. Holy cow! Talk about tossing a sticky note onto the mangoes! Just like we are all at different parts on the spectrum of our OCD, we are all at different parts of our exposure therapy journey and what *we are willing* and able to do. My method may not be your method. But I encourage you to find your method. If I can do it, you can do it. You can find your way, and you will find your way.

I hope that this book can be a good resource for you like the book *Brain Lock* was for me.

I'm aware that the book WILL NOT BE PERFECT. I'm sure there will be typos, I could have offended somebody, and I'm sure I'll think of things I would've liked to have said differently. There's no doubt that I will have more thoughts to share with you. But that's good. I will collect them on scraps of paper until next time, my friend.

I've found that forgiving others and holding no one prisoner for their trespasses is freeing and that no one else is responsible for my happiness. I will never achieve perfection, the ghost I used to chase around moment by moment. I will never say I am perfect and I am done and that I am a fully frosted and decorated cake. It won't happen in this lifetime. Will I ever live in a Mr. Clean world, like the made-up worlds that I see on TV? Nope. Do I have to redirect my mind throughout the day, even quite possibly while doing yoga and meditation? Yes! However, is mental stillness more available to me than ever before? Yes! Do I wish you peace and mental stillness? You betcha!

Chimpsay can always say, "Let's freak out!" And I can always say, "Not today, Chimpsay, not today."

I once heard that life is full of waves, and we can determine which to surf. I am a believer of this way of thinking.

Life is like a carnival in many ways, and OCD is like a circus. I choose which rides to go on and which rides not to go on. I no longer ride the Zipper, nor do I need to. I choose to leave the OCD Circus; there are just too many other great things to do.

And when I am on a plane, I spend more time looking out the window and am honored when I get to feel amazement and fascination when I look at the clouds. I don't need my hand puzzle anymore.

My friend from college told me a story about her father when he was in the military. When it was lunchtime, the guys would sit inside the tent and eat their sandwiches. The flies were unbelievable; they were everywhere and would constantly land on the sandwiches. The guys who had been there for a long time would just ignore the flies. They could always tell who the new guys were because they would be busy swatting the flies off their sandwiches.

Chimpsay and the ruckus he makes are like the flies at times. I just keep doing life the best I can—keep eating the sandwich. It's weird; the more you ignore the flies, the happier you become.

Loving the flies on my sandwich, well now, that's a stretch! But maybe I will get there; you never know!

It has been great sharing this time with you; thank you for allowing me to do so. You, my friend, are not alone. Life is messy; we all have pain and frayed ends and stuff that we're working on.

You have an inner light and are radiant; I can see you from here.

It's time to avenge what you lost! *Dum vivimus vivamus!* (Let us live while we are alive!) Let's do this!

As for the future,
your task is not to forsee it,
but to enable it.

Antoine De Saint Exupery

> Obsessive Compulsive Disorder (OCD) is a disorder of the brain and behavior. OCD causes severe anxiety in those affected. OCD involves both **obsessions and compulsions** that take a lot of time and get in the way of important activities the person values.

Common Compulsions

WASHING AND CLEANING

- Washing hands excessively or in a certain way
- Excessive showering, bathing, tooth-brushing, grooming, or toilet routines
- Cleaning household items or other objects excessively
- Doing other things to prevent or remove contact with contaminants

CHECKING

- Checking that you did not/will not harm others
- Checking that you did not/will not harm yourself
- Checking that nothing terrible happened
- Checking that you did not make a mistake
- Checking some parts of your physical condition or body

REPEATING

- Rereading or rewriting
- Repeating routine activities (examples: going in or out of doors, getting up or down from chairs)
- Repeating body movements (example: tapping, touching, blinking)

- Repeating activities in "multiples" (examples: doing a task three times because three is a "good," "right," "safe" number)

MENTAL COMPULSIONS

- Mental review of events to prevent harm (to oneself/others, to prevent terrible consequences)
- Praying to prevent harm (to oneself/others, to prevent terrible consequences)
- Counting while performing a task to end on a "good," "right," or "safe" number
- "Canceling" or "Undoing" (example: replacing a "bad" word with a "good" word to cancel it out)

OTHER COMPULSIONS

- Putting things in order or arranging things until it "feels right"
- Telling or confessing to get reassurance
- Avoiding situations that might trigger your obsessions

Common Obsessions in OCD

CONTAMINATION

- Body fluids (examples: urine, feces)
- Germs/disease (examples: herpes, HIV)
- Environmental contaminants (examples: asbestos, radiation)
- Household chemicals (examples: cleaners, solvents)
- Dirt

LOSING CONTROL

- Fear of acting on an impulse to harm oneself
- Fear of acting on an impulse to harm others
- Fear of violent or horrific images in one's mind
- Fear of blurting out obscenities or insults
- Fear of stealing things

HARM

- Fear of being responsible for something terrible happening (examples: fire, burglary)
- Fear of harming others because of not being careful enough (example: dropping something on the ground that might cause someone to slip and hurt him/herself)

OBSESSIONS RELATED TO PERFECTIONISM

- Concern about evenness or exactness
- Concern with a need to know or remember
- Fear of losing or forgetting important information when throwing something out
- Inability to decide whether to keep or to discard things
- Fear of losing things

UNWANTED SEXUAL THOUGHTS

- Forbidden or perverse sexual thoughts or images
- Forbidden or perverse sexual impulses about others
- Obsessions about homosexuality
- Sexual obsessions that involve children or incest
- Obsessions about aggressive sexual behavior towards others

RELIGIOUS OBSESSIONS (SCRUPULOSITY)

- Concern with offending God or concern about blasphemy
- Excessive concern with right/wrong or morality

OTHER OBSESSIONS

- Concern with getting a physical illness or disease (not by contamination, e.g. cancer)
- Superstitious ideas about lucky/unlucky numbers or certain colors[1]

---

1 Adapted from the IOCDF.com website. Reprinted with permission by the International Obsessive Compulsive Foundation.

Your OCD Kung Fu Dance Moves

· · · · · · · ·

KEY POINTS TO REMEMBER

· · · · · · · ·

Practice and visualize your steps!

1. Accept

2. Focus

3. Identify

4. Breathe and **Pause**

5. Greet

6. Stay Aware

7. Agree

8. Remember

9. Forgive

So you feel choppy on the dance floor do you?
Don't worry practice will get you there. Where?
Your freedom! It's worth all the effort and more.

ACKNOWLEDGMENTS

I see this body of work like a colorful woven tapestry. Many people have had an influence either on me or on my work directly. I would like to take this opportunity to show my boundless gratitude.

Thank you to all the talented people at Red Wheel/Weiser/Conari for believing in this project and contributing your time and expertise in many various ways through the book publishing process.

My deep, heartfelt appreciation goes to Dan Kalb, PhD, and Pam Schweitzer, APRN-BC.

Dr. Kalb, you were there for me when I felt most lost, exposed, and vulnerable. When I was completely in the dark as to what was going on with me, you gave me a flashlight. You encouraged me to get outside of my OCD prison and showed me the way. Thank you for helping me understand OCD and for encouraging my wellness of being. You have always been supportive of my creativity and writing and are a big part of why this book gets to exist. Thank you.

Pam, you have an uncanny ability to get to the real issues and just pass by the BS. Over the many years you have offered many ideas, and I have enjoyed applying them to my daily life with positive results. You taught me that I may not be able to control what goes on outside of me, but I can control what goes on inside of me. And you have showed me this with your warmth and understanding. You have challenged me to keep growing. You have given me your guidance and practical ideas on how to build my inner warrior and keep going strong even during the tough stuff.

I would like to acknowledge and thank my dear friend Morgan. You generously gave your time and your editing expertise to this project. Thank you for openly sharing your ideas and enthusiasm and jumping right in. Your contributions were instrumental in giving form and direction to the book, especially in its earliest stages. Your belief in the project combined with your help was inspiring. I am forever grateful.

Caroline Pincus, I thank you for your faith and enthusiasm in the book and giving me the room and time I needed to create it. Your mad editing skills and guidance were invaluable to the project moving forward and really taking flight. You are a wonderful book midwife—smart, supportive, and knowledgeable. Thank you for helping me through the book publishing process and for getting me out of the woods and back on the narrative path time and time again. We were terrific book partners, and I feel blessed to have met and shared time with you.

I would like to give a big thank you to my mentor, Bernie, who showed up at a critical time in my life. You were my spiritual traffic guard, and I am grateful and still amazed how the universe opened up and brought us together. You and your guidance are two big reasons that I am here right now living a healthy life. You were so right: it's all about doing the dance.

My sincere gratitude goes to these book authors and mentors: Dr. Wayne W. Dyer, Dan Millman, Jeff Bell, Dr. Rick Hanson, Dr. Michael Jenicke, Eckhart Tolle, and Tara Brach. Thanks for the wonderful books that you've created and put out into the universe. They're soulful, insightful, and full of positive energy and great ideas. Your spirit combined with the many thoughts that you've shared through your work have made an impact on me very personally. You're my inspiration and my heroes.

I would like to give an extra shout-out to Rick Hanson and Jeff Bell. Thank you for your guidance during the creative process of this book, including having faith in the project and believing in my artistic vision. You're both incredibly busy people, contributing so many great things to humanity, and I thank you for the valuable and gracious time that you've shared with me.

I have to turn the clock back and thank these four significant and special people in my life: outstanding teachers Earl Bitoy and Chris Davis, and friends to the end, Cal and Judy. As sappy as this might sound, it was through your eyes and your actions that you reached me, especially when I was a kid trying to find my way. It's as though *you each told me that I was okay and that everything would be okay* even though I was very unsure of that myself. You are the definition of a safe place to land.

I would like to acknowledge the many creative souls who created the wonderful artwork that is placed throughout this book. Most of you I never got a chance to meet in person; however, I have met you through your artwork. I have enjoyed finding ways to share the meaningful vintage ephemera that I have gathered to communicate different feelings and emotions throughout this book. Thanks to my incredibly talented and patient husband, Doug; thanks for teaching me and reminding me the way to get something done is to chip away and stay the course. Thank you for the expressive drawings and artwork that you made for this project, including the cover. Thanks, Joseph Allen Black, for contributing your tremendous and thoughtful design skills, and for going on this sometimes challenging ride of making a book with me. Artist extraordinaire Doug Horne, thank you for letting me share two of your beautiful paintings with the readers. For years I have told you, "I'm making a book. I'm making a book. Just you wait and see." You were always so positive and believed me. A special shout out to the multi-talented artists Shawn Dickinson and Mark Thompson, for jumping into this project and creating some expressive art that really adds something to the story. John Matthews, fellow author and brother-in-law, thanks for your encouragement and direction with making this book the best that it could be. Thank you to my dear friends, Victoria Moran, and Mitch O'Connell. Thanks for complementing and rounding out this project with your photographic contributions. Kim and Candy from Rosebud Antiques, in Countryside, IL. Thanks for providing me with a ladder and allowing me the freedom to take pictures of all the interesting monkeys in your fine store. Oh, so many years ago and here we now are.

Thank you to NPR for the first public service announcement that gave valuable information about OCD and for being the first place we ever heard the words *obsessive-compulsive disorder* strung together. Thank you to all the people who make up the International OCD Foundation (or IOCDF). You are an incredible resource for those suffering with OCD and their loving family members and friends.

I also would like to acknowledge my extensive Retro-a-go-go! family. You gave me the space and support that I needed when I had my "book hat" on and not my "retro hat" during the entire process of creating the book (which seemed to go on for a very long time). Thanks for jumping in and doing whatever needed to be done to keep the business thriving. I have to give a shout-out to some particular Retro-a-go-go! Gals: Eryn, Janelle, Lauren, Heather, Anna, Jen, Michaela, Maekena, and dear Marie. I cherish the special times that we have shared together. To my dear friend Jen, thanks for being there with Doug and me during the great times and the challenging times. I'm always amazed by your natural talents and many contributions. A special thanks to Maekena for all the early mornings and late evenings you put in with me while organizing the book and moving it forward. You are a trooper and I appreciate you so much.

I'd like to show my heartfelt gratitude to my family and friends. I appreciate your understanding when I said, "I've got to get off the phone right now; I've got a book to write."

I want to thank the long, flowy-haired chiropractor in Walnut Creek who told me to *go eat some ice cream and have some fun*. As it turns out, that's not such a bad idea after all!

FURTHER RESOURCES

Bass, Ellen, and Laura Davis. *The Courage to Heal: A Guide for Women Survivors of Child Sexual Abuse, 4th ed.* New York: HarperCollins, 1988.

Bell, Jeff. *Rewind, Replay, Repeat: A Memoir of Obsessive-Compulsive Disorder.* Center City, MN: Hazelden, 2006.

Bell, Rob. *Love Wins.* New York: HarperOne, 2012.

Brach, Tara. *Radical Acceptance: Embracing Your Life with the Heart of a Buddha.* New York: Bantam Dell, 2003.

Burns, David D., MD. *Feeling Good: The New Mood Therapy.* New York: Avon Books, 1999.

de Becker, Gavin. *The Gift of Fear: Survival Signals.* New York: Little, Brown and Company, 1997.

Dyer, Wayne W. *Wishes Fulfilled.* Carlsbad, CA: Hay House Inc., 2012.

Glass, Lillian. *Toxic People.* New York: St. Martin's Press, 1997.

Gunaratana, Bhante Henepola. *Mindfulness: In Plain English, Updated and extended ed.* Somerville, MA: Wisdom Publications, 2011.

Hanson, Rick. *Hardwiring Happiness.* New York: Harmony, 2013.

Hanson, Rick. *Just One Thing: Developing a Buddha Brain One Simple Practice at a Time.* Oakland, CA: New Harbinger, 2011.

Hanson, Rick. *Buddha's Brain: The Practical Neuroscience of Happiness, Love, and Wisdom.* Oakland, CA: New Harbinger, 2009.

Harris, Dan. *10% Happier.* New York: HarperCollins, 2014.

Hershfield, Jon, and Tom Corboy. *The Mindfulness Workbook for OCD: A Guide to Overcoming Obsessions and Compulsions Using Mindfulness and Cognitive Behavioral Therapy.* Oakland, CA: New Harbingers, 2013.

Hibbs, Stanley, PhD. *Anxiety Gone: The Three C's of Anxiety Recovery.* 2007.

Kasl, Charlotte Davis, and Lenore Davis. *Finding Joy: 101 Ways to Free Your Spirit and Dance with Life.* New York: Harper Collins, 1994.

Jampolsky, Gerald and Diane V. Cirincione. *Change Your Mind Change Your Life: Based on A Course in Miracles.* Glen Ellen, CA: Bantam Books, 2009.

Knapp, Caroline. *Drinking: A Love Story.* New York: The Dial Press, 1996.

Mathew, Hal. *Un-Agoraphobic: Overcome Anxiety, Panic Attacks, and Agoraphobia for Good.* San Fransisco: Conari Press, 2014.

Millman, Dan. *No Ordinary Moments: A Peaceful Warrior's Guide to Daily Life.* Tiburon, CA: H J Kramer Inc., 1992.

Millman, Dan. *Way of the Peaceful Warrior: A Book that Changes Lives*. Tiburon, CA: H J Kramer Inc., 2006.

Murphy, Terry Weible. *Life in Rewind: The Story of a Young Courageous Man Who Persevered Over OCD and the Harvard Doctor Who Broke All the Rules to Help Him*. New York: HarperCollins, 2009.

Prather, Hugh, and Gerald Jampolsky. *The Little Book of Letting Go*. Berkeley, CA: Conari Press, 2000.

Schwartz, Jeffrey M., and Beverly Beyette. *Brain Lock: Free Yourself from Obsessive-Compulsive Behavior*. New York: HarperCollins, 1996.

Stout, Martha. *The Sociopath Next Door*. New York: Broadway Books, 2006.

Tolle, Eckhart. *A New Earth: Awakening to Your Life's Purpose*. New York: Penguin, 2005.

Toms, Michael, and Justine Toms. *True Work: Doing What You Love and Loving What You Do*. New York: Bell Tower, 1999.

RESOURCES FROM
THE INTERNATIONAL OCD FOUNDATION (IOCDF)

Brosh, Allie. *Hyperbole and a Half: Unfortunate Situations, Flawed Coping Mechanisms, Mayhem, and Other Things That Happened.* New York: Touchstone, 2013.

Callner, James. *The Touching Tree.* Awareness Films. Awareness Foundation for OCD. *www.afocd.org/films/the-touching-tree/.*

Cunningham, Bess, and David Michael Lyndon Thomas. *OCD and Me: My Unconventional Journey Through Obsessive Compulsive Disorder.* Liverpool, UK: PlantaPress, 2014.

Dumont, Raeann, and Aaron T. Beck. *The Sky Is Falling: Understanding and Coping with Phobias, Panic, and Obsessive-Compulsive Disorders.* New York: W. W. Norton, 1997

Grayson, Jonathan. *Freedom from Obsessive Compulsive Disorder: A Personalized Recovery Program for Living with Uncertainty.* New York: Penguin, 2004.

Lakeside Center for Behavioral Change. *Information about Compulsive Hoarding.* Fargo, ND, *www.lakesidecenter.org/video.html.*

Mulcahy, Kristen. Live OCD Free—Your Personal Pocket Therapist app. *www.liveocdfree.com/.*

Neff, Kristin. *Compassionate Body Scan Audio Tape.* Louisville, CO: Sounds True, 2014.

Neff, Kristin. *Self-Compassion: The Proven Power of Being Kind to Yourself.* New York: HarperCollins, 2015.

Shackman, Lynn, and Shelagh Masline. *Why Does Everything Have to Be Perfect?* New York: Dell, 1999.

Headspace app. Los Angeles: Headspace USA. *www.headspace.com/how-it-works.*

Wilson, Reid. *Strategic Treatment of Anxiety Disorders* (6-Video Series), *www.psychotherapy.net/video/Strategic-Treatment-Anxiety-Disorders*

Wortmann, Fletcher. *Triggered: A Memoir of Obsessive-Compulsive Disorder.* New York: Thomas Dunne, 2012.

ABOUT THE AUTHOR

Photo: Doug Pagacz

KIRSTEN PAGACZ is the founder of Retro-A-Go-Go, an online seller of retro kitsch. She suffered from OCD for two decades before discovering that it had a name (and a cure). Before founding her own company, she worked in marketing and sales for a number of Fortune 500 companies. She is a member of the International OCD Foundation and won first place in one of their art competitions.

TO OUR READERS

Conari Press, an imprint of Red Wheel/Weiser, publishes books on topics ranging from spirituality, personal growth, and relationships to women's issues, parenting, and social issues. Our mission is to publish quality books that will make a difference in people's lives—how we feel about ourselves and how we relate to one another. We value integrity, compassion, and receptivity, both in the books we publish and in the way we do business.

Our readers are our most important resource, and we appreciate your input, suggestions, and ideas about what you would like to see published.

Visit our website at *www.redwheelweiser.com* to learn about our upcoming books and free downloads, and be sure to go to *www.redwheelweiser.com/newsletter* to sign up for newsletters and exclusive offers.

You can also contact us at *info@rwwbooks.com*.

Conari Press

an imprint of Red Wheel/Weiser, LLC
65 Parker Street, Suite 7
Newburyport, MA 01950

www.redwheelweiser.com